DATA SCIENCE
JOBS

Career Guide for Students & Professionals

ANN RAJARAM

For career advice, datascience project guides and other questions, please visit
www.journeyofanalytics.com

This book is dedicated to my wonderful husband, Rajaram Kumar, for being the anchor of my life!

Thank you for being such a staunch supporter and honest critic; this book would not have been possible without you!

Table of Contents

SECTION A – INTRODUCTION

Ch 1. INTRODUCTION

Welcome to the world of data-science!

Every day we see and hear about how "Data science" is the most high-paying career pathway that is transforming every industry from healthcare to manufacturing to agriculture. CEOs are quoted as eager to hire data science professionals at all levels. Yet, applicants spend weeks and months learning these skills, applying to hundreds of jobs, and… SILENCE.

So where are the jobs? How do you get started?

How do you get a data science job?

How do you become a data-scientist, data analyst or data engineer?

This book aims to answer this burning question and help you land a full-time well-paying job in this exciting field. This books cuts through the generic resume advice and gives practical advice on where the best jobs are, and how to get to an interview stage. Over the last few years, I've advised and successfully helped dozens of friends, relatives and friend-of-friends land a lucrative job in the data science field, even though I am NOT a recruiter. So, I can vouch that these tips work!

1.1 WHO should read this book?

- If you have spent countless hours applying to dozens of data analyst or data science jobs online and have received zero or no job offers.
- Women, looking for analytics roles after a career break, including spouses on H-4 EAD.
- Students (including F-1/ OPT visa international students) close to graduation who are eager to get a job.
- Experienced technology professionals looking to pivot their careers into this lucrative domain.
- You recently completed a datascience coding bootcamp or online certification but are unable to land interviews.
- Data science enthusiasts looking to apply their courses in a real-world corporate job.

- You have a child, husband or other close relative who is struggling to get an analytics job and would like to help.

1.2 I am just getting started / looking to get started?

- If you are just exploring the datascience realm and/or if you do not know at least one among R, Python or Tableau then please start with section A & B and chapter 4 from section C. This will help you approach your studies from a practical skill-building perspective. You can come back to the job search and interview Qs in section C and section D later.

1.3 Who should NOT start this book?

- If you desperately need a job and/or money in the next week, then put down this book and look elsewhere. Even if I set you up for an interview tomorrow, (and no one can do it so fast) the hiring process in most companies is at least a month long. Most people take 2 to 3 months to get hired.

- You are not willing to tailor your resume, work on the strategies in this book, and basically put in the hours to make your profile look irresistible to hiring managers.
- You only believe books with 100,000 words or longer. Job searchers don't need a thesis, they need quick actionable items to help them get started in their career. This book is deliberately kept short and concise with no fluff. This will help you read quickly and get ahead in your job search.

1.4 Book Layout

The summary below gives you an idea of what to expect in the coming chapters:

1.4.a Section B – Learning and Skill building

- ***How to become a Data Scientist*** –High level learning plan to establish yourself in the datascience field.
- ***Resources for Technical Skills*** best websites and reputed links where you can learn programming skills for advancing your career.

- ***Profiles that get hired*** – please, do not skip this chapter. If your online profile and resumes are truly stellar, this chapter will validate it. If not, the tips will help you get hired faster.
- ***Where are the jobs?*** - Baltimore is full of healthcare analytics; Calgary caters to oil industry and streaming analytics, while Detroit is full of startups. Different locations and industries have slightly different job requirements. Knowing these can help you mount a targeted campaign, or at least set more realistic expectations.
- ***LinkedIn*** - This chapter focuses solely on LinkedIn, with strategies other than hitting the default "Apply" button.
- ***Twitter*** – This site is rarely used as a job-hunt resource, which is why you can steal a march over other jobseekers.
- ***Networking*** – Nothing beats old-fashioned connections. This chapter will help you identify and leverage connections that you did not know existed and meet with the folks who can get you hired.

- ***Upwork*** – Build your portfolio and start earning within a week. Most people fail to utilize Upwork and are disappointed when they do not make any money. This chapter will give you the correct tips to start earning on this wonderful platform.
- ***Good Old Search*** – This chapter lists many niche sites, and websites with job postings. Apply the tips you learned in the previous chapters to make the most of these sites.

1.4.c Section D - Interview Preparation

- ***Interview Process***
- ***Interview Qs***
- ***Some more advice*** – For more Qs and topics not covered in other chapters.

Final disclaimer, all the strategies in this book have been tested successfully for dozens of folks, but only in the US and India. This proves these principles are suitable for multiple job markets, but not necessarily all markets. There are exclusions to every rule, so please do not consider this book to be legal advice, and tweak accordingly.

1.5 Job Search Action Plan

If you already have technical skills, then skip right on to section C which deals with the job search aspects.

- **Action #1** - Read chapters 4 and 5, i.e. "profiles that get hired" and "where are the jobs" to polish your resume and profile. If you need to start earning or show employment (F-1 students, for example) then navigate to the chapter on Upwork.
- **Action #2** – Start with LinkedIn to apply to the jobs with the best chance of getting hired.
- **Action #3** – Work on the job search strategies using the chapters on Twitter, search, networking. LinkedIn is still the largest marketplace for jobs, but the others are good supplements, to increase your chances.

1.6 How long will it take me to get a job?

Nothing in this life is guaranteed, especially not a job. The market could crash tomorrow and hiring freezes could impede your goals. An old friend could decide to return a favor and hire you tomorrow!

However, assuming nothing major changes in your life and the economy, and you have the necessary skills, we will assign 1 week for tasks related to polishing your profile itself and the job research. Actual job matching using LinkedIn and Twitter with the strategies listed in this book will last 2-4 weeks. Ideally, you should start receiving feedback from recruiters and managers in 10 days or so. The hiring processes in most companies take at least 4 weeks, to receive an offer letter, starting from the day you receive an HR or introductory call.

Assuming you will do your personal branding and social media postings in parallel, most folks have seen results in 2-3 months.

1.6 Bonus Content

Please note that I will be periodically be updating this book with bonus content based on changes in the market for datascience employment, frequently asked questions and more. So, remember to check back into this book for new content, tips and strategies. All bonus material will be added to chapter 14 – "bonus content".

You can also sign up on my website where I send out monthly emails with new project tutorials and other updates on the book. {Note, the signup link = http://bit.ly/2Znwjw4. Or navigate to the Projects page via https://www.journeyofanalytics.com/projects-1.html and use the sign up link on the top, beneath the menu bar. }

Without further ado, let us get started…

SECTION B – LEARNING & SKILL BUILDING

Ch 2. HOW TO BECOME A DATA SCIENTIST

This question and its variations are the most searched topics on Google. As a practicing datascience professional, and manager to boot, I personally get this question dozens of times every week. This chapter is my detailed answer.

Note, the title says data scientist, but the information remains valid for any datascience-related job such as data analyst, data engineer, machine learning engineer, BI analyst, etc.

2.1 Coding & ML skills

You need to master programming in either R or Python. If you don't know which to pick, go with R or toss a coin. If you are familiar with MATLAB, SPSS or SAS then you should pick R. If you took basic programming with Python, then the choice is quite clear. Once you master one language, you will find it quite easy to pick up the other. As you move higher in your career, you might be placed in teams where the other language is popular, so you will eventually have to learn both.

When I say master, you need to know more than writing a simple calculator or "Hello World" function. You should be able to perform complex data wrangling, pull data from databases, write custom functions and apply algorithms, even if someone wakes you up at midnight.

By ML, I mean the logic behind machine learning algorithms. When presented with a problem, you should be able which algorithm is suited for which case, its advantages and disadvantages. You must know how to write the code snippet for all these algorithms.

2.1.a Where to learn?

- The best sites are Coursera, Udacity and Udemy, in random order. There are countless others, but these 3 are my favorites.
- Datacamp is good especially since they offer custom career paths like Coursera, and the monthly subscription allows you to do as many courses as you like.
- I do know some folks who did the nanodegree from Udacity, and they got excellent help in the job search process akin to large universities. However, even the nanodegree is a longer time

commitment compared to sites like Udemy or Coursera.

- *My absolute favorites* are the courses on Udemy from Kirill Eremenko (no affiliation)

If you are still stuck on which to choose, I would suggest learning basic R and data visualization from Coursera (JHU) and then moving to the Machine learning fundamentals from Kirill's course on Udemy.

2.1.b Should I go for a masters or graduate degree?

This is tricky. If you are outside the US, then an international degree is one way of legal immigration. However, the costs are steep, and you lose the ability to earn for 2 full years. Plus, immigration laws are getting tougher, so job competition is high. Remember to count the lost opportunity of earning as well as the risk of market saturation by the time you graduate.

If your employer is offering a partial or full educational reimbursement for tuition costs, then an additional degree is a good idea. But check if you can truly balance the time commitments since online degree courses are as rigorous as full-time classes and it might take you longer to graduate if you space out classes too much. Most employers also expect a reasonable grade (A or B) or else the reimbursement does not apply.

Unless the college is Stanford, MIT, Harvard or other Ivy League, then the college reputation does not really matter much to employers. What will help you (once you finish the course) is how well you can present your skills and convince a potential employer that you deserve a spot on their team at a large salary.

Personally, if you can get the skills from cheaper alternatives like Udemy then go for it! Remember to link the completion certificate to your LinkedIn profile. Most employers do consider it on par with certification courses offered at local colleges.

If you are debating between an MS in analytics and an MBA, I would suggest looking at the curriculum and speaking to recent graduates about salary ranges. If you are already working and have 5+ years of experience, then an MBA would be better as you can move to managerial roles or product owner roles. For experienced hires, entry-level data scientist roles typically do not offer a huge jump in salary.

2.2 Build your portfolio.

Unfortunately, the data science realm is getting overcrowded. The best way to get the attention of recruiters and hiring managers is by having a unique online portfolio. Recently, many companies now request GitHub and website links on online applications, so a portfolio helps. Many also start technical interviews by asking candidates to present a project of choice and sending a GitHub link.

The best way to showcase your value to potential employers is to establish your brand via projects on GitHub, LinkedIn and your website. If you do not have your own website, create one for free using WordPress or Wix.

2.2.a Stumped on what to post in your project portfolio?

- Start by looking in the kernels portion on the Kaggle site www.kaggle.com There are tons of starter scripts and free datasets available. Try your hand with the code and then apply it to a new dataset.
- Enroll in any active competitions and navigate to the discussion forums. You will find very generous folks who have posted starter scripts and detailed

exploratory analysis. Fork the script and try to replicate the solution. Check your standing on the leader board. Then tweak the code and see how your ranking changes. Learn by doing.

- **Recommendation** – start with the titanic and Ames housing prices dataset and then work your way up to image recognition and text processing.

- My professional website Journey of Analytics [www.journeyofanalytics.com] also houses many interesting project tutorials, including Twitter API usage, text analytics, map visualizations, and many more. Navigate to the Projects main page to sign up for monthly updates via email when new projects are added.

- Try Upwork via www.upwork.com . Upwork is a fabulous site to get paid gigs you until you get hired full-time. At the same time, you can modify the same projects and add to your portfolio. Having freelancer experience on Upwork is a fabulous way of being unique and standing out to potential employers! As a recruiter once told me, "it is easier to hire someone who already has a job, than to evaluate someone who doesn't!"

2.3 Apply for jobs strategically.

Please do NOT randomly apply to every single analytics job in the country. Be strategic using LinkedIn to reach out to hiring managers. Remember, it is better to hear "NO" directly from the hiring manager than to apply online and wait in eternity.

Competition is getting fierce, so be methodical. The next few chapters in this book will help you pinpoint the best jobs in your target city and connect with hiring managers for jobs that are not posted anywhere else.

If your first job is not at your dream company, do not despair. Earn and learn. Every company, big or small, will teach you valuable skills that will help you get better and snag your ideal role next year. I do recommend staying at roles for at least 12 months, before switching, otherwise you won't have anything impactful to discuss in the next interview.

2.3.a Mothers returning to work

- It is sad that brilliant women are penalized for taking care of young kids. My personal peeves aside, what did work for mothers I know is to accept the first role you get, preferably at a small firm, stay 6 months and then move on to better roles. The starting pay might not be what you expect, but it is still better than no salary at all.

- Startups are great too, as you can learn multiple skills and then jump couple of levels at your next gig. Just ensure you are not expected to do tons of overtime without compensation.
- The first job will be hardest to get, so do not give up hope easily. Most women will find a job in under 4 months.
- Remember the skills that helped you be a super mom, wife and homemaker will also help you shine once you land that first job.
- Look for women-only hiring events. Many large employers hold annual events to increase diversity in tech. Ask around in your friend and family circle and look for local event news.

2.4 Continuous learning.

Even if you've landed the "data scientist" job you always wanted, you cannot afford to rest on your laurels. Keep your skills current by attending online classes, conferences and reading up on tech changes.

My favorite resource is Udemy (*again*). Network with others to know how roles are changing, and what skills are valuable. Read business magazines like Forbes and Wall Street Journal and subscribe to e-newsletters to follow trends in your domain.

Going to conferences is extremely beneficial. Yes, the good ones are expensive when you add travel and lodging, so enquire if your company has discounted passes. If not, think of it as an investment in yourself.

You can also follow me on Twitter @anu_analytics as I regularly post articles and retweet latest news on datascience topics.

Ch 3. RESOURCES FOR LEARNING TECHNICAL SKILLS

There are many resourced freely available on the internet on how to get certified in various programming languages for datascience and related software. In this chapter, I am presenting only those resources which I have personally used and recommended or sources where I could verify that the content was excellent.

This book does contain a dedicated chapter on 100+ interview questions on statistics, machine learning and logic. I deliberately do not cover technical programming questions on R/SQL/Python and Tableau since you need to have solid hands-on practice for most of them. Instead this chapter provides links to sites which specialize in interview questions on those topics.

3.1 SQL

Despite the hype about Mongo DB, Hadoop and non-relational databases, normal SQL tables are not going away anytime soon. Plus, Python/R/Tableau all connect to SQL servers, so being able to write decent queries is a crucial skill whether you are a data analyst/ scientist/ reporting analyst.

Only academic projects link to static .csv or Excel files. In the real world, you will connect to a regular Oracle/SQL server/ Amazon Redshift database. So, having strong SQL knowledge is a very useful and mostly mandatory skill.

Some datascience roles also have a SQL evaluation round along with Python coding tests, so better to pick it up sooner than later.

3.1.a SQL coding resources
1. w3schools - https://www.w3schools.com/sql/

This site is completely free and has an online editor to practice SQL queries.

Once you are done, you can test your skills by taking an online quiz.[Link = https://www.w3schools.com/sql/sql_quiz.asp] If you know some basics of SQL, take the quiz first and then you can refresh only the sections where you are rusty. I love this site because I can quickly read through the concepts to refresh myself before an interview.

2. Codeacademy - https://www.codecademy.com/

They have a separate specialization targeted at business analysts, but the curriculum is good for any data science role. Please note, the starter course is free, but some projects are only available to paid subscribers. Still it is quite cost effective because you can take a paid subscription for a month, get the certification and then cancel the membership.

The membership is for all courses, so essentially you could complete the Python and "data science" path for the same flat fee.

3. Datacamp - https://www.datacamp.com/

This one is a good starter course and like Codeacademy the flat fee covers all courses. If you already have a subscription, you may want to use the course from here. Otherwise I found the curriculum to be similar to w3schools, so you might as well as choose the free site (w3schools).

4. Textbook - Learning SQL: Master SQL fundamentals

This is a classic and comprehensive textbook from O'Reilly that serious SQL users, including database administrators swear by. However, unless you have access to a sandbox or SQL server in office you cannot practice the concepts without returning to a site like w3schools. Some public libraries do hold a copy, so you can look if it is available or buy a used copy.

ISBN-13: 978-0596520830
ISBN-10: 9780596520830

3.1.b SQL Interview Qs

Typically, SQL interview Qs involve writing a short snipped of code to pull data, so the resources listed above should help. However, useful set of Qs are listed in the links below:

- Conceptual Qs from geeksforgeeks - https://www.geeksforgeeks.org/sql-interview-questions/
- 100 SQL Qs and answers - https://www.softwaretestingmaterial.com/sql-interview-questions/

3.2 R Programming

I covered my favorite sites in Chapter 2. However, listing the links here for easy reference along with cheatsheets to help you brush up on concepts.

3.2.a Coding resources for R:

- The R programming course from Coursera is a great way to start if you do not want to spend moolah on the entire specialization path via https://www.coursera.org/specializations/jhu-data-science
  - In all fairness, I did complete the Data products course (part 9) and

practical machine learning (part 8) courses way back in 2015 when the course was just launched.

- Once you know the basics, look at Kirill's comprehensive course on machine learning from Udemy. This particular course (via https://www.udemy.com/machinelearning/) has code scripts in both R and Python. Effectively, you can master 2 languages for the price of one.

- If you need a textbook for the mathematical background and code for machine learning algorithm, then refer to the award-winning book "Introduction to Statistical Learning" by Gareth James, Tibshirani. They do offer a free MOOC and pdf in case you want to check it out which is also listed in the link above.

- Another textbook that I have personally used and adored is Hadley Wickam's "R for Data Science". Hadley is Chief Scientist at RStudio and a member of the R Foundation, so this is the R-Bible for serious programmers.

3.2.b R interview Qs

- Tutorials point has a comprehensive list of Qs - https://www.tutorialspoint.com/r/r_interview_questions.htm
  - This site also provides code snippets and tutorials so it can be considered a FREE alternative to a basic introductory course in R However it does not have full-blown scripts so students might find it difficult to know how to put all the syntax together. Hence not including it as a learning resource.
- www.Intellipaat.com has a list of 100+ questions on R.
  - Some of these are simply explanations to functions. A few are extremely obscure functions which you will rarely use in real life. So don't feel discouraged if you think you do not know half the answers.
- Practice using RStudio. If you've done due diligence and created a strong portfolio, you will not need to brush up

on these skills. Refer to chapter 4 for
more details.

3.3 Python programming

3.3.a Coding resources for Python

- Kirill's course again, as mentioned in the
  R section. Link to comprehensive course
  on machine learning from Udemy.
- Udemy course from V2 Maestros, called
  "Applied Data Science with Python".
  (Link = https://www.udemy.com/applied-
  data-science-with-python/) This does
  cover basic statistics and some data
  engineering concepts which will be
  helpful to folks from non-technical
  backgrounds. Otherwise stick to Kirill's
  course.
- If you need a textbook, then the best
  resource is "Python for Data Analysis"
  by Wes McKinney.

3.3.b Python interview Qs

- Guru99 has a list of questions related to
  main Python concepts –

https://www.guru99.com/python-interview-questions-answers.html.

- Edureka has a list of 100 interview questions - https://www.edureka.co/blog/interview-questions/python-interview-questions/.
  - Some Qs are conceptual, while others are code-based.
  - This site also offers tutorials and paid certifications in R. The site is quite popular in India and has excellent reviews online. However, I don't know anyone personally who has used the site so not including as a programming resource.
  - In all fairness, the interview questions are excellent. If we judge the site on that basis, it seems like a resource on par with DataCamp.
- TutorialsPoint - Good list of Qs and the code snippets come useful to prepare before a coding interview (live / take home test/ online exam) Link = https://www.tutorialspoint.com/python/python_interview_questions.htm

- Techbeamers – I had never heard of this site until very recently. Love the topic-based quizzes as it tests your concepts and programming skills. My Python skills have become a bit rusty since my office and personal projects are primarily coded in R. So, I was happy to use this site to refresh my Python knowledge. Link = https://www.techbeamers.com/python-interview-questions-programmers/

3.4 Tableau

I don't need to emphasize the importance of Tableau, now that Salesforce has acquired it and proven how valuable this tool is to users and enterprises. What I will add is that it is a great tool for setting up self-service analytics, recurrent reporting and exploratory analysis. Even if you do know coding and mainly work on model development, this tool can help you create stunning dashboards. Use it to create a compelling story to convince senior management to take action on your insights.

3.4.a Tableau learning

- Honestly, nothing beats the videos and resources on the site itself. Link = https://www.tableau.com/learn/training
- Second best is the Udacity data visualization course. Link = https://www.udacity.com/course/data-visualization-in-tableau--ud1006 True you will need to pay for the course, but from a hiring/ employer perspective the certificate is highly respected and comparable to a Data Associate certificate from Tableau itself.

3.4.b Tableau interview 3Qs

- Vizard.co – from Sateesh Kumar who is a Tableau architect and genius viz Expert, based in Australia. He wrote a short post on LinkedIn which invited so many comments (4000+) and page views (~ half million) that he decided to write a dedicated blog post about it.
- Edureka – This site pops up again so feel free to bookmark the main site.
- Mindmajix – 100 Qs on Tableau. Half seem to be very basic which will likely never be asked in a real interview. However, if you don't have much project experience in Tableau then it is a good

site to get started.
https://mindmajix.com/tableau-interview-questions

- Intellipaat – another useful site you may want to bookmark.

3.5 Machine Learning Algorithms:

- At the cost of sounding repetitive, use Kirill's Udemy course and the book by James Gareth et al. (refer back to R-programming section)
- If you want a quick refresher on algorithms, then look at this infographic provided by Microsoft. Link = https://docs.microsoft.com/en-us/azure/machine-learning/studio/algorithm-cheat-sheet
- SAS also provides some excellent reference material that clearly shows which algorithms should be applied for what scenario. Link = https://blogs.sas.com/content/subconsciousmusings/2017/04/12/machine-learning-algorithm-use/
- IBM has a fantastic pdf (FREE) on their site that you can use. Just read chapter 3 for a quick overview. Link =

https://www.ibm.com/downloads/cas/GB8ZMQZ3

3.6 Statistics

- If you took probability and statistics courses in your undergrad, then you just need a decent refresher. If you plan to read the textbook by Gareth then you do not really need additional guidance.
- However, if you did not have any introduction to statistics or feel as if you do not recollect anything, then download this free pdf book from deAnza College. It is the most comprehensive book on statistics that I've seen in a while. https://openstax.org/details/books/introductory-statistics
- Introduction to Statistics is another fantastic book by Dr. David Lane from Rice University. The book might seem excessively long at ~700 pages but it is written in an easy manner and can be read almost like a story book. Yes, a mathematics book that is enjoyable to read. Link = https://open.umn.edu/opentextbooks/textbooks/introduction-to-statistics

Just pick one resource each and try to develop a good understanding those concepts. You will need to keep referring to them. As you practice, the concepts will become clearer and help you write better code, which will help you become a more valuable employee.

SECTION C - JOB SEARCH

Ch 4. PROFILES THAT GET HIRED

No one boards an international flight without a passport and appropriate visa/travel documents. Airport security will simply bar you at the gate. Similarly, unless you showcase a "hire-worthy" profile you will be weeded out by human and electronic application tracking systems.

4.1 What makes a stellar profile?

These are basic attributes that need to be fulfilled before any hiring manager will even look at your resume. They don't guarantee a job by themselves, but not having them means rejections are a certainty!

- **LinkedIn profiles:** A LinkedIn profile rated as "All-star". This is an auto-generated adge that indicates your profile is completed with all relevant details. So, your name should crop up when a potential employers or recruiter searches for a suitable candidate. We will go into more details in the sections below.

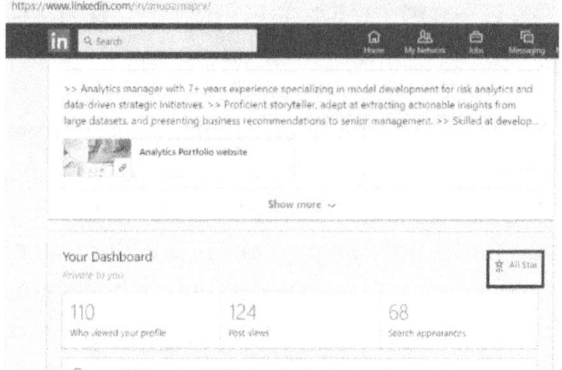

- **<u>Professional website:</u>** Data science roles are essentially technical roles, so a personal website is a must.
    - ○ If you don't have any, create a FREE, simple blog on WordPress and write about your learning journey. Sites like WordPress and Wix have made it super easy, so there is no excuse not to have one.
    - ○ Connect it to your GitHub profile with code files. If you don't already have one, please do create a GitHub profile! Many employers are now mandatorily asking for GitHub links so don't wait for an employer to ask before creating one. In most cases, the lack of one might put you out of

the running, before you even know you were considered.

- o Add links to your personal site and GitHub to your LinkedIn profile.

- **"Smart resume"**: A resume that highlights what you can do for potential employers in the top half of the first page. Managers are busy, and you want to make sure that your resume interests them enough for a second look. No one has time to read through even 2 pages of resume, so the first half page should scream that you fit their criteria. More on this later.

- **Strong programming skills:**
  - o Data analyst - R/Python or SAS programming. SQL is a bonus since most Fortune 500 companies still rely on relational databases. Data visualization in R, Tableau or Alteryx. Basic machine learning principles and applications.
  - o Data scientist – All the skills for data analysts plus, machine learning algorithms, deep learning, Hadoop.

- Data engineer – Python, ETL skills to build and maintain data pipelines. Experience with Looker and equivalent.
- These are the very basic skills without which you are going to get rejected. (Sorry for the harsh reality check!) If you don't have mastery over these, then please look at sites like Udemy and Coursera to get started.
- Projects with a summary page. If you don't have any, create some. A word or pdf doc (or markdown file, if you want to get fancy) should summarize in 1 page about the project – problem statement, tech stack used, analysis insights and conclusion. Data analysts and data scientist need to showcase their recommendations to senior managers, so the summary doc is a great way to show you can do all parts of the "job".

4.2 LinkedIn profiles

There are many excellent articles on what makes an amazing LinkedIn profile. A condensed version based on profile sections is listed below. All these sections must be mandatorily filled in:

- LinkedIn profile is a must, and your profile and photo must be visible to public. Until you get your dream job, data privacy will have to take a back seat. Sad, but true. Also fill out your experience and education details.

- Profile picture must be professional. Photos give a personal connection, so they must be visible to the public. You are applying for a job in data science, not reality TV.

- **Connections:** You need a fully completed LinkedIn profile with at least 500+ connections. If you just completed your undergrad, then you may be able to get away with only 300+ connections. Any less and it looks like you don't socialize well which raises suspicions that you may not be a team player. Only CEOs, billionaires, tenured professors and senior executives get to live with an incomplete or non-existent LinkedIn profile. Reach out to all your classmates, friends, family, neighbors, import your contacts. Do what you need to; but increase your connections. This will also ensure the odds that someone in your extended network will be the hiring manager who will offer you a job. It also will help you look up relevant posts, discussed in the LinkedIn chapter 4.

- **Recommendations:** Have at least 3 recommendations. If you don't have any, ask classmates, friends or family to give you some. Write a 50-word recommendation template for them, so they don't need to think too much.

- **Projects:** List at least 3 projects related to data science, preferably in different domains. It is perfectly acceptable to describe academic projects or codebase you tweaked from an online course. Don't copy/paste proprietary code, though. Add links to codebase files from your personal website and GitHub. You can get inspiration from the kernel scripts on Kaggle.com scripts and my website www.JourneyofAnalytics.com

- **Skills:** These skills act as SEO keywords for your profile. So, when someone is searching for a data scientist, then

LinkedIn's algorithms include these to decide who to push up the top. Each endorsement that you get for your skill helps your chances further, and endorsements for skills by experts will help you bubble up higher.

- Choosing skills, however, is tricky and is different based on your target role, company and domain. However, to start with, log in to LinkedIn and type in "data scientist <dream company>" in the LinkedIn search bar. Select "People" if it is not selected. I've used Google as an example as shown in image below:

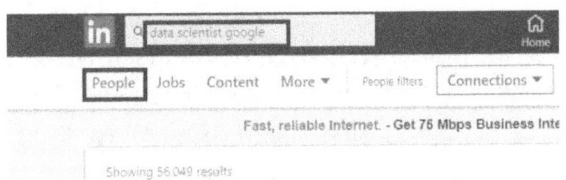

- Look at 5 profiles who have worked at this company for at least 18 months, and then look at the skills they have listed. You will notice some skills get repeated on all the profiles or are modifications of the same thing. Make sure these skills are listed in your profile, but only if you have them. If you don't then try to gain those skills as quickly as possible.

- o Repeat for 3 target companies. If your job search has geographical constraints, then add city names in the search bar. Add skills on your profile based on your research.
- o Reach out to your network and get endorsed for those skills. If your network has someone who has 20+ endorsements for that skill, then specifically request them to endorse you.
- o Note, before you send out requests for endorsements, make sure those skills are listed as the first 5 skills. Otherwise folks must unnecessarily look through your 50 allowed skills and most will abandon the task. LinkedIn sorts skills based on a default order of date the skill was added, and which ones you are most endorsed for, so you will have to manually re-order your skills.

This is annoying, but unfortunately necessary. [I don't have any proof this is how LinkedIn algorithms work, but the technique has worked for me, and for all the folks who made modifications following my advice]

- **<u>Headlines and summary:</u>** LinkedIn will display your most recent job title and industry as the default headline, but that is a waste of SEO power, especially if you had a break in your career or are pivoting from another stream.
  - o Choose a headline based on the role you are looking for, and please do not state "Actively looking" or "open to opportunities". I've heard mixed opinions on this, but unless you are a student, advertising you are unemployed and unable to get a job only seems to hurt your chances. Err on the side of caution, and don't show desperation on LinkedIn.
  - o Use the summary tab to write a succinct description of your skills and the value you bring to the

table. My current profile
screenshot is listed below:

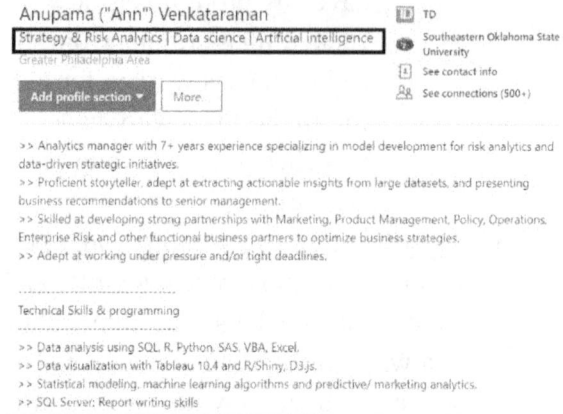

- **<u>Certifications:</u>** LinkedIn allows you to export certificates from several online learning sites, including Udemy, Coursera, Udacity, EdX, and many others. Worst case, you can manually enter the certifications, and attach links to the image. (Host images on your personal website, GitHub or Google Drive).
  - These certifications act as testimonials for your skills, and as keyword matching. I once got a message from a recruiter who was looking for Hadoop expertise in the area, even though I'd only learnt it in my spare time. I passed

50

on the job, but it was interesting to know that certifications pushed me up in the search listings.

Once you've filled out all these sections, your profile should be marked as "all-star" and increase the "searchability" of your profile. Look at how your "public" profile looks to others and make changes as appropriate.

Next, the acid test – type "data analyst" (or your preferred job title) in the search bar and then filter for your location. Scroll through the names and titles of the results. If your profile is not visible in the first 5 pages, then either you are in a saturated market (San Francisco), or your profile still needs some editing, or both. If you are not in the first 5 pages, and your profile is all-star, then do not worry too much. This limits the number of searches you will feature in, so you may receiver lesser messages from hiring managers. You can overcome this point, by using the search strategies in the following chapters.

4.3 Smart Resumes

Resumes can be functional, chronological or hybrid. I personally prefer the "hybrid" version, as it presents the details most relevant to the job I am applying. Unless you have 10+ years of experience, the "hybrid" resume will fit your needs.

- Note, multiple recruiters and clients have hired me (and my protegees) on the strength of our "hybrid" formats. So, the format works.
- Occasionally, managers or HR personnel will come back to me asking for a chronological format. I always comply because the purpose of the resume is accomplished, i.e. getting noticed by the hiring decision-maker.
- US recruiters often expect resumes to be 2 pages or less. Mine is 4 pages, but the hybrid format ensures that I've never received any complaints. Only ton of job offers!
- Notice how the format clubs job functions together, rather than job titles. Titles and work history time frames have been relegated to the end, under work history. This deliberate format ensures managers who look at the resume read

the most important details at the very
beginning.

- Even if you have very little experience,
you should be able to describe your
academic projects using this format.
- Tweak the "objective" based on your
career goals.
- Do not lie or fabricate on your resume.
You will be found out!
- If you completed your LinkedIn profile
adequately, you will have enough content
to create such a resume.

4.4 Sample Resume

My personal resume screenshot below: (some
parts truncated)

Anupama ("Ann") Puthur Venkataraman
████████ ██ Ph. 20█████

OBJECTIVE

Proactive analytics professional looking for managerial roles where my analytics programming and consulting skills can help deliver data-driven business solutions to accelerate growth!

Excellent communication and presentation skills, from working directly with clients, senior stakeholders, vendors and multiple lines of business.

SKILLS

Programming	Tableau, R, SQL, Python, SAS, C/C++, HTML, Unix, SAP-ABAP, VBA, Advanced Excel user.
Project Management	MS Project, Clarity, JIRA, Trello, Shiny and Excel Dashboards, business reporting.
Analytics	Hadoop, Machine learning, predictive modeling, financial modeling.

FUNCTIONAL EXPERIENCE:

Data Science / Analytics

- Develop fraud monitoring models and strategies to mitigate the fraud loss while balancing customer experience, operational and product P&L impacts.

- Implement real-time rules for card transactions in TSYS, VBV (Verified by Visa) and internal decision engine.

- **Ranked Top 10%** in Kaggle competition for creating highly accurate predictive model for calculating customer satisfaction and churn for Santander Bank.

- **Scoring models** – Create segmented scoring model for cloud-based behavioral assessment tool and user profiling for mobile dating app.

- **Text and Social media analytics** - Designed and implemented Twitter analysis web-tool for in-house storage and analysis of change in Twitter Follower Counts for media client.

- Advanced analytics using machine learning algorithms (Random Forest, Classification, regression and clustering methods) and REST API programming.

- Owner and blogger at www.journeyofanalytics.com

Financial and Strategy modeling:

- Financial modeling to understand ROI from implementing fraud strategies for new product campaigns, as well as evaluating vendor scoring models.
- Use risk analysis models to identify pricing change resulting in **$30,000 increase in revenue** per month.
- Create new financial plan to improve collection strategies for urgent care clinic, for pending bills and to reduce future defaults.
- Design/maintain billing simulators for verifying updates to accounting systems based on pricing changes.

Project management:

- **Lead dashboard development** and fraud monitoring for new online authentication tool used with digital marketing campaigns.
- **Develop implementation roadmap** for cloud-based behavioral assessment tool, including cloud architecture plan, high level **database design schema, infrastructure** cost and resource planning, security considerations for enterprise client users, etc. **Work with client COO and Microsoft Azure team** for first phase of software implementation.
- Lead cross-functional team **for critical datacenter upgrade project** at BlackRock. Completed project rollout 1-month before schedule across 3 datacenters, with seamless transition and zero impact to clients.

Client Relations/ Communication Skills:

- Present results and recommendations from data analysis to senior management.
- Coordinate with BlackRock client relationship managers, internal and client-side technical teams throughout implementation cycle and maintenance SLA period.
- Technical contact for SAP functional experts (FiCo, CRM, BW modules) at Infosys.

EDUCATION

BE (Electronics), PIIT, University of Mumbai, India. (Honors)

MBA Finance, Southeastern Oklahoma State University. (in progress)

WORK HISTORY

May 2014 – Mar 2015. **Analyst**, BlackRock Inc.

Aug 2012 – Dec 2013. **Lab instructor & Teaching Assistant,** University of Delaware.

Mar 2009- Jan 2011. **Systems Engineer**, Infosys Technologies, Ltd. India (multiple offices)

CERTIFICATIONS

- Foundations of Business Strategy, Udemy.
- Credit Risk Modeling in R, DataCamp.
- Foundations of Marketing Analytics, Coursera.
- Taming Big Data with MapReduce and Hadoop, Udemy.
- Inbound marketing certification, HubSpot.
- Google Analytics Individual Qualification.
- Developing Data Products, Coursera.
- Operations Management, Udemy.

AWARDS

- Ranked Top 10% worldwide Kaggle Santander (analytics) competition.
- 1 of 10 worldwide IEEE Travel grant recipients, to attend 5-day IPS Conference at Bellevue, WA. (2013)
- Excellence award by client for Top Performance, Novartis SISNET/Infosys Pune.
- Emerging Leader certificate for completing Blue Hen Leadership Program, UD.

VOLUNTEER WORK & EXTRA-CURRICULARS:

- Women Initiative Network (WIN), Philadelphia Chapter, Nasdaq.
- Office Volunteer, DVI Materials Resource Center.
- Lab instructor, E&R department, Infosys-Pune campus.
- Co-Editor, "Gurukul" – company-wide magazine for new recruits at Infosys.

Please use this format to tweak your resume. It will take time, but it is completely worth it. If you feel you need professional help with your resume, then please consult Upwork or Fiverr for those type of services. Note, my resume is listed under the "Resources – Career Resources" page of my website under the header "Career Guidance". My website is www.journeyofanalytics.com

Ch 5. WHERE ARE THE JOBS?

Do you know "**WHERE**" you would like new job to be?

Unless you are married, most people do not have a valid answer for this, especially students who are close to graduation and are willing to relocate anywhere.

5.1 Why location matters

Sadly, location does matter, because companies in specific industries tend to concentrate in specific cities. For example, healthcare and defense research companies in the Baltimore area. Salary range, skill requirements and even job titles (some companies use data analyst and data scientist titles intermittently) will also be different.

In large banks or fintech startups, "data analyst" jobs could be listed under different titles like reporting analyst, credit analyst or even "associate". One of my colleagues at Nasdaq was titled "pricing specialist" even though he was coding and working on data analysis tasks.

On the practical side, many managers simply do not have the budget to have candidates flown in for in-person interviews and may not be interested in paying for relocation costs.

Job market research is, therefore, crucial before you start applying.

5.2 Job Market research

The job market research in the section below will help you identify the best roles in the area and indicate if you need to expand your area of search or look for a different title.

If you are a student, with no specific favorites, pick SFO and another 2 cities like Chicago or Philadelphia. Yes, all are in different corners of the country. If you don't have a preference, then SFO is the best bet, despite the high living expenses. It continues to be the largest hotbed of data science jobs because of the concentration of companies like Google, LinkedIn, Microsoft and a plethora of startups. Not to say it is the only city with lucrative jobs – other major cities like Charlotte (NC), Philadelphia, Baltimore, NYC, Dallas, Chicago, Detroit, Denver also have multiple opportunities. But SFO is a good starting point.

Now, let us start on the market research portion:

1. Open LinkedIn and navigate to the jobs section. Type "data scientist" in the keyword bar, and target location in the "city" bar. If you live in a city close to another larger city, then choose the larger city. For example, if your target city like "Wilmington, DE", then choose "greater Philadelphia" instead since we are still in the research phase and want a broad selection.
    [In case, you are not familiar with job search in LinkedIn, the image below indicates navigation for the jobs (1), keyword bar (2) and location search bar (3)]

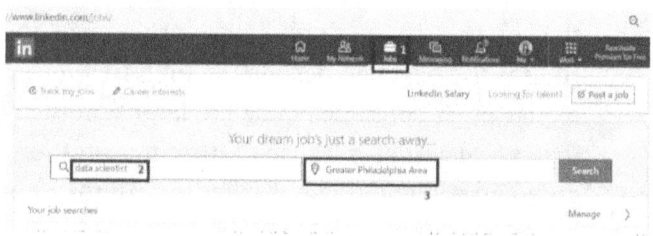

2. Once you get the initial search results, select (a) date posted tab on the top left, and then (b) choose past month.

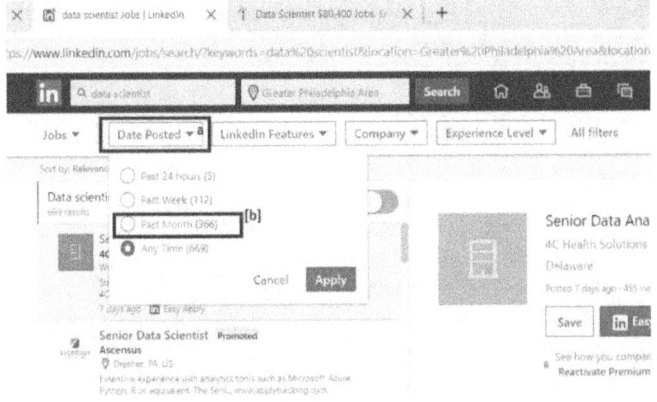

3. Note the number of results it returns and scroll down through the company names. As seen from the image below, there are 366 results for the Philadelphia area, and the top results are all big banks in the Wilmington, DE area, fintech roles from KPMG, Deloitte, as well as the larger employers in central Philly area like KPMG, UPenn Medical centers and Comcast.

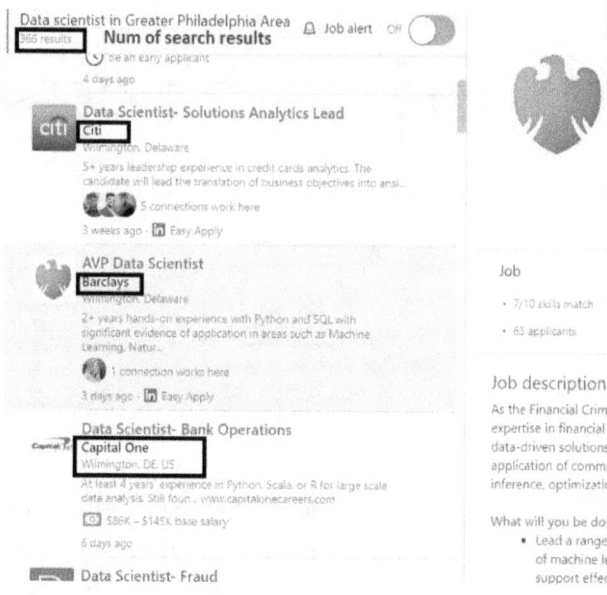

4. Click on the job roles and read through the job requirements, to see patterns in skill requirements and experience requirements. If most roles need 7+ years and you only have 3, you are going to be passed over, although you may have a shot with 5 or 6 years. If the roles all call for Python+Hadoop and you prefer R, then you will need to master Python.

5. Repeat for "analytics" in the search bar, and same target geography. This will expand the search and show you roles

with alternate job titles, if any. You will also notice companies you may have not known existed in the area, or that interest you immensely.

6. If you live in a smaller city, say Oklahoma, then the results will be less in number (17) and you will notice the skill requirements are more in tune with data engineers and database analysts than reporting analysts. In this case, be mindful that it will either take longer to find the right role, or you need to expand your search

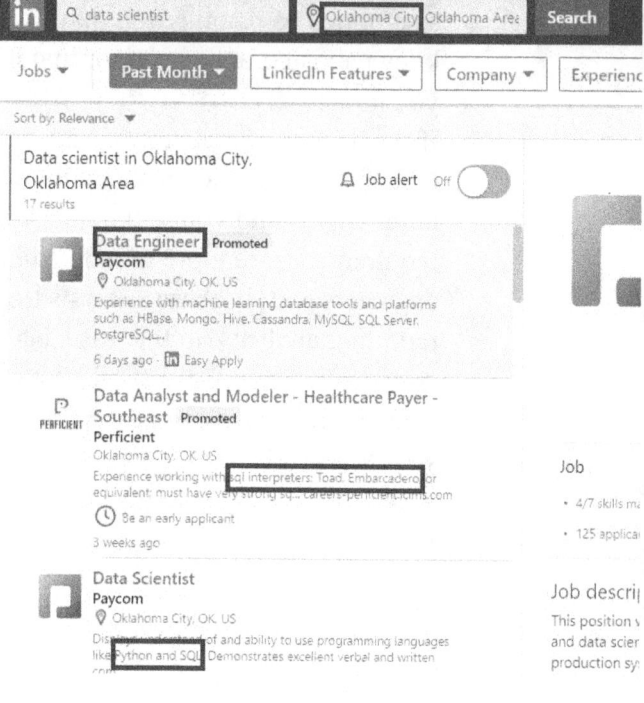

7. Use the skills from this research to
    update your resume and be sure to add
    them in the "skills" section under your
    LinkedIn profile. Also make note of all
    the job titles and companies; we will use
    them in the next chapters. DO NOT
    APPLY; not yet.

8. Repeat the same on Indeed.com and make notes of the company names, titles and skills.
9. Navigate to glassdoor.com and get the salary range. Note, living expenses differ by location, so an $80k salary in Philadelphia is worth more than $95k in SFO or Boston. If you are an experienced employee, transitioning from a different domain or role, and the salary feels like a step down, check if you would qualify for a more senior or managerial role.
10. For salary ranges, use Glassdoor.com look at the national averages first and then salary for your nearest geographic location. This will be the range you can reasonably expect. Personally, I've found Glassdoor to be remarkably accurate, compared to sites like Payscale.com or indeed.com. For readers in Canada use glassdoor.ca, glassdoor.in for India. For others, use the corresponding link for your country.

5.3 Action Items

a. Choose a target city, identify and update profile with skills and create list of top 2 job titles for the roles in the area.

b. Recognize salary ranges for your target role in the area you expect to work.

Ch 6. LINKEDIN – CREATIVE WAYS TO STAND OUT

LinkedIn is the leader of all job search sites, and one which I've personally found the most profitable. Unfortunately, simply using the "apply" button on job postings does not work for most candidates. And if you see a button named "apply on site" then please refrain, your resume is going to end up in the cyber-world black hole called application tracking system, never to be heard again. Don't be fooled by the auto-generated acknowledgement emails from LinkedIn or the parent company.

Personally, I would rather hear "NO" from a manager than wait indefinitely with zero feedback.

Instead be strategic and use LinkedIn to connect directly with the gatekeepers and decision-makers using the strategies below.

6.1 Job posts from content tab

This is one of the best and most under-used methods of finding a great job on LinkedIn. Instead of applying to LinkedIn jobs, you will directly reach out and respond to original job posters.

Here's how you do it:

1. Remember the job titles and location you so painstakingly researched from the previous chapter? Well type them in the search bar of the home page and choose "content". An example is shown below for data scientist Dallas.

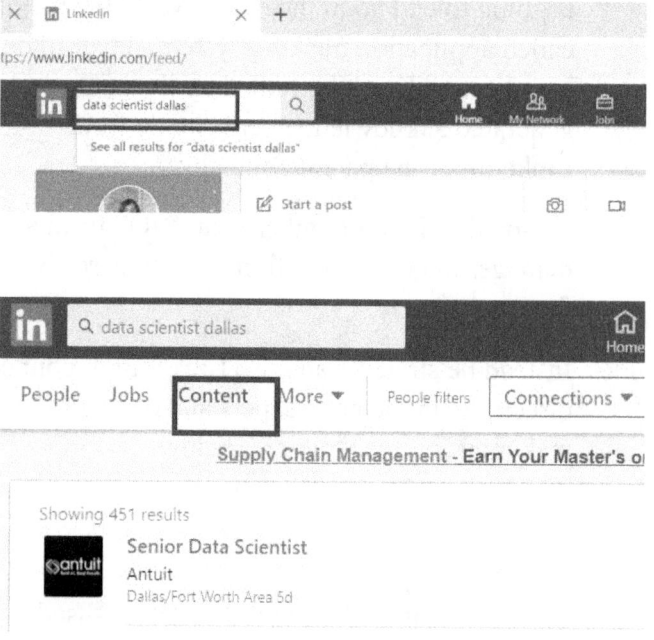

2. Once you get the results, select "past week" from the date posted dropdown options. Content posts for jobs tend to get filled very quickly, so don't waste time with stale results.

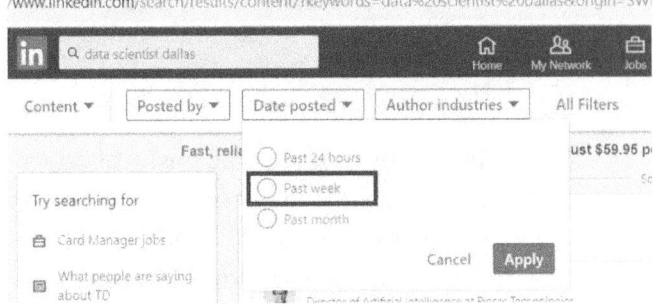

3. Now scroll down through the results for the most relevant posts. Typically, the top few will be actual job posts from the hiring manager which someone in your network has liked/commented or re-posted. Note, this was why having large number of connections helps, as you can use these posts to connect with the decision makers.

[Note, names of actual people have been hidden, to adhere to privacy concerns.]

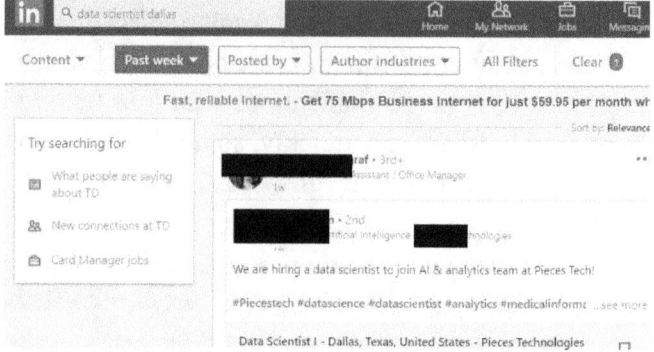

4. In the above image the post was added by one of my 2nd level connections and re-posted by a 3rd level connection. If I were a candidate interested in this role, I have 3 options:

   a. Like the message. Useful but does not indicate my interest in the role. The hiring manager is not a mind-reader, and most people don't get a notification unless a post reaches 50+ likes.

   b. Comment on the post, saying something along the lines of "interested". This is passive, and I now am forced to wait for the poster to look at my profile, check whether I am a fit and answer back. Some job posters are proactive and will respond, but

the wait may be agonizing. This
option is also useless if I want to
keep my job search a secret.

c. Best option. Click on the original
job poster and send an invitation
with the following message
template:

"Hi XXX,
Saw your job post for a data
scientist at Pieces Tech. Would
love to connect and learn how
my skills can help your org.
Best wishes, Candidate."

99.999% of LinkedIn users will
accept, irrespective of whether
they are open networkers or not.
If the contact accepts, but does
not respond within 2 days, then
look up their email from the
LinkedIn profile and send them
an email with the sample text
below:

"Hello XXX,
Thank you for accepting my
LinkedIn invite to connect.

Saw your job post for the data
scientist position at Pieces
Tech. Would love to learn
more and discuss how my skills
might be of use.
Best wishes, Candidate."

Use the same template to send them another LinkedIn message as well.

d. I am not going to provide any follow-up items on this because I've had 100% success rate with this method. This "direct contact" always gets back a response. 95% of the time, the response is to ask for a resume via email or set up an introductory call over the phone. The rest 5% has been feedback to say the role is filled up or I am not a good fit. If you receive the latter, thank the person for their feedback with good grace, and reply that you are ready to help them in the future.

e. In case it so happens, that you do not receive a response via this method (unlikely, but possible) then look up another person from

the same company and repeat, if
you truly love the company.

5. Rinse and repeat for other posts in the
original search. Some may have specific
constraints such as contractual position
only, or a clause saying no F-1 allowed.
If the constraint puts you out of the
running, then don't message the recruiter
to argue the point. For example, if you
are not happy with contract roles, as
shown in the image below, then accept it
and move on to greener pastures.

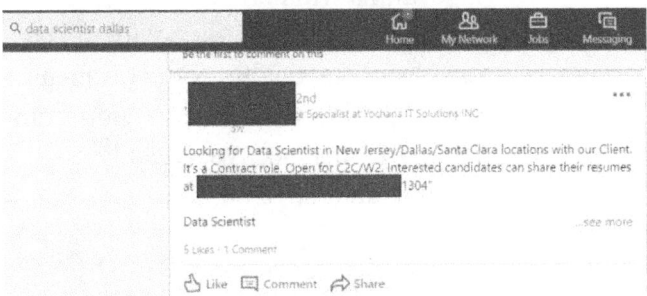

6. **Note, this method is highly manual, but
it is also why it seems to work with
such high accuracy.**

7. Second point to remember is that this
search will also show lots of posts you
don't care about, as a job-hunting
candidate. For example, you may notice
posts from recruiters trying to snag a job

for the candidates on their books. Skip the post to more relevant ones.

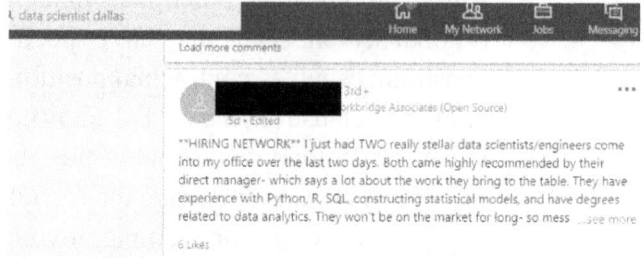

8. Some posts maybe from recruiters with multiple open role. So, LinkedIn algorithms will combine the "data scientist" and another job with the target city. Mathematically, correct from a search perspective, but annoying from a job search perspective. Quickly read through and move on.

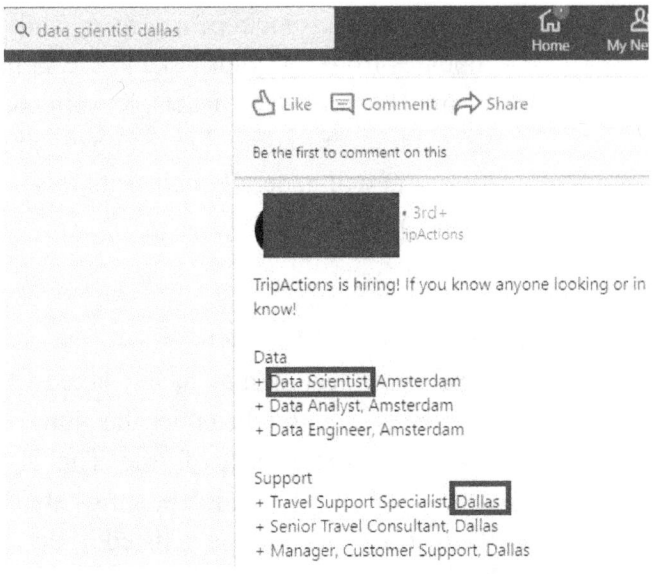

9. Do not ignore posts from recruiters or agencies. They get paid if you do get placed, so it is a win-win for both. They can bypass online application tracking systems and get your resume directly to the hiring manager's desk, so do NOT scoff. Most will also offer valuable tips on how to frame your experience to best advertise you to the manager, advice on interviews, keep you updated on timelines, and basically be your wingman for this process.

10. You will see some repeated roles, and updates from different folks in the same team. Ignore the duplicates. Keeping an Excel tracker to note role, company and contacts will generally help with this issue of duplicates.

6.2 Roles with recruiter names

Now the previous section may have coaxed you to believe that LinkedIn jobs under the "jobs" sections are a complete waste of time. That is only partially true. LinkedIn job postings are useful if the job poster's name is listed. [See image below]

Note, the following:

- "Apply" button indicates that you will NOT be redirected to the company website.
- 1 of my connection works here, so I could ask them for a referral.
- The job poster name and profile are visible.

Here's what you can do:

- If you can see both recruiter name and referral connections, connect directly with job poster first. Like the previous sub-section, invite to the job poster directly, but tweak the message to say that (a) you are interested and have applied to the role, (b) you would love some feedback. Remember to customize your resume when you apply.

- If the job-poster name is missing, but you have connections, then look them up. Do you know them personally? If the answer is yes, email or message them to ask if they will refer you internally. This step will only work if the referral is someone you know from school, college or previous work. If the contact is someone you only met online, and have never spoken, then please do not make this request. Internal referrals require that this person log in their company intranet, fill your details and put their employee number as referee. Unless they know you, they will not be willing to risk their professional reputation. Saying yes to LinkedIn connections is one thing, but referrals are a big commit. When in doubt, don't do it!

What about job postings with no connections – no referrals or visible job posters? Simple use the company name, job title and go back to the LinkedIn search bar on the home page. Use the earlier method to get a direct connection to the job poster. Again, having a simple Excel tracker helps a lot. Create a list of companies and job roles. Then use them in the search bar and scroll through to get people's names. If you cannot see a similar content post in the first 5 pages, move on to the next role. You can look up a recruiter, using the method in the next section. Once you gather all the names, send messages with slight customizations.

6.3 Connect with recruiters in your target companies

You probably have a list of 10 target companies. If you don't have such a list, create one.

If you did not find names of job posters in the previous section, then this strategy will help.

Using the search bar on the LinkedIn homepage, type the company name and technical recruiter, and select "People" on the search results.

There are some ***boutique recruiting firms*** which only specialize in tech jobs and some which only work on filling "Datascience" roles. It is a great idea to connect with such folks. Some will openly tell you that they do not work on entry-level roles but will accept your invitation anyway. In that case, do not despair. These recruiters' LinkedIn feeds might include open roles from others which is a good fit, so connecting with them has zero downside.

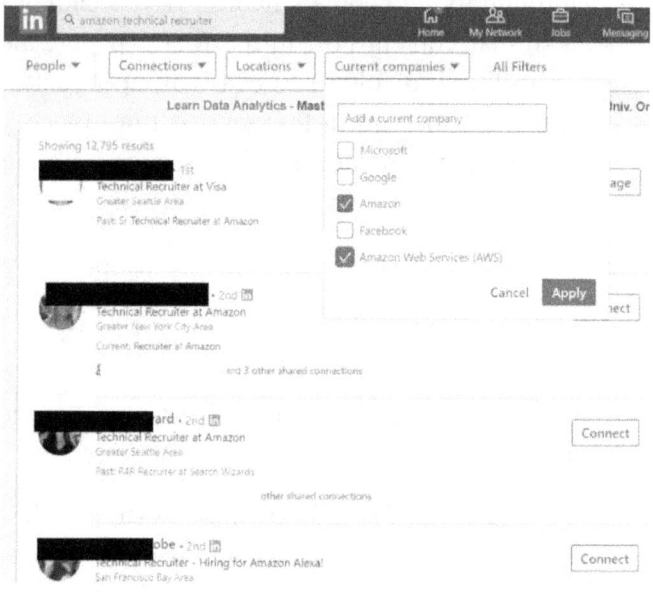

You may need to select "current company", as you may see search results of names who were previously at this company. See the image above, where the first name is a recruiter from Visa, not Amazon.

Message them using the template in the first section.

If you are a student, either current or just graduated, then you can also search with the phrase "<company> campus recruiter".

Warning: I have noticed that LinkedIn will sometimes show me only 2-3 pages of search results and then expects me to upgrade to a paid account to view more results. These many results are generally enough, but if you want to view more, logout and come back after an hour or so. If the problem persists, clear your cache.

Groups

LinkedIn groups have sadly become quite noisy, with everyone trying to establish their authority or spamming with sales pitches. However, they can be a good resource for job seekers, if you have the patience to scroll through the clutter. You might want to use the "find" command [Ctrl+F] with the phrase "hiring". Somehow adding the job roles seems to make the search invalid.

Note some groups have totally banned job postings. So read through the group rules, which are typically listed on the extreme right of the group homepage.

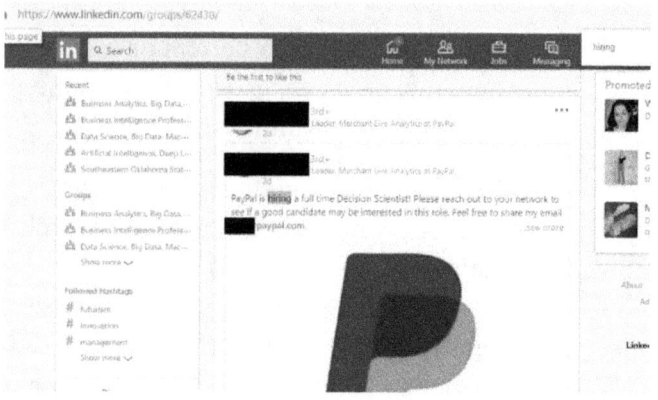

This chapter should have given you enough leads to start looking for relevant jobs. Ideally, you should see 10+ new leads per day.

Short interruption …

Did you like the book so far? If so, please leave a review on Amazon using ASIN number B07S4P8GGY. It will help other jobseekers make progress on their job search to gain the job of their dreams.

If you do not have time to write a long review, feel free to simply state that you found the book useful. You do have the option of editing your review at a future date.

I personally read every email and review, so your feedback will be appreciated to improve this book further.

Thanks, Ann.

P.S.: Simply navigate to Amazon and search "Data Science Job in 90 days". This book should be the first link. Click on the ***** indicating reviews. You will be taken to a page with a button named "Write a Customer Review".

Ch 7. TWITTER FOR JOB SEARCH

Although Twitter is not as big or popular as LinkedIn, it is still a great resource for job leads. On the plus side, most people rarely use Twitter for job hunting, so there is lesser competition. Plus, there are job aggregator bots that you can follow to receive leads. However, you won't find as many leads as you might on LinkedIn, especially for smaller cities.

In the following sub-sections, you will find strategies to use Twitter to find job leads:

7.1 Twitter search

This is very similar to what you did for LinkedIn. First, type "data analyst <City>" and hit Enter. On the initial search results, click on "Latest" on the top left, as the default sorting is "top" i.e. tweets with the most engagement (retweets, likes and comments). The search filters are not useful for narrowing down our criteria.

You'll notice most of the jobs are by job aggregators, but if you scroll down far enough, you will see a couple of job posts by real recruiters and managers. See image below; name hidden for now, for privacy reasons.

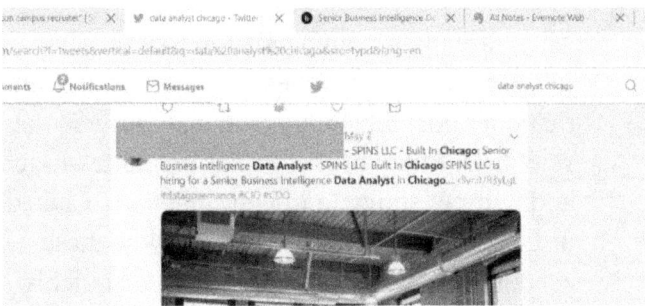

However, please be mindful of the date of the tweet, as the search will often become quite old, depending on the search volume. Another point to note, is that some of these tweets will list roles and companies that you may not know existed on any other job board.

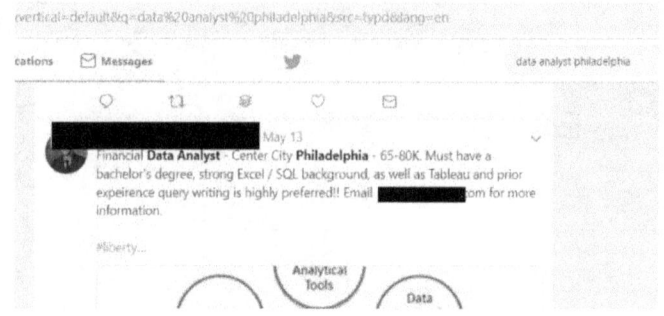

Note, for some cities it is more useful to use
"analyst <city>" than "data analyst" or "data
scientist". Try different iterations for your target
city.

7.2 Follow recruiter and job-aggregator bots

These are my recommendation for datascience
job bots on Twitter. These are Twitter accounts
that only post jobs related to analytics and data
scientists. Many of these roles are quite unique
and will not show up in your inbox via LinkedIn
or Glassdoor. So, remember to follow these
accounts. Sadly, these roles get filled quickly so
remember to look frequently and only apply to
recent postings.

- @DataScienceSHA
- @KaggleCareers
- @KDnuggetsJobs
- @allStartupJobs

- @Jobs_Statistics
- @RJobListings

In addition to the above list, do not forget to follow me on Twitter at @anu_analytics, as I do re-tweet interesting datascience jobs that are sent to me or ones that show up on my feed.

7.3 Bonus content - Other Search Tips:

- Some folks who are not recruiters, have started to post jobs with the tag #DataScience and/or #rstats. These are generic tags, so you will have a lot of content, but it is worth a try.

- R-bloggers [handle - @Rbloggers] post jobs in a monthly roundup post, occasionally at random too! As the title suggests, the site is targeted to programmers specializing in R, but the job posts are not exclusively so. Many jobs do allow the option of R/Python.

- If you are from humanities, social sciences or bioinformatics then Twitter does have some cool listings. For example, some screenshots below of roles in May:

We're looking for a community-focused, problem solver that loves data to help build @CityofMiami's analytics program. Spread the word! #DataScience #Innovation #ETL #OpenData #DataCleaning #Dashboards #CivicTech #Analytics #RStudio #PowerBI #DataModeling
forms.office.com/Pages/Response ...

@PaulCampbell91

We're expanding the data team at Epicentre-@MSF and are looking for R programmers/developers to help us build production quality packages and apps.

If you're interesting in applying your R skills to major humanitarian projects - apply below! #rstats

Epicentre is looking for a R Programmer (M/F) in Paris, France
BackgroundEpicentre is increasingly using the R programming language to

- Here is another one from Chicago Museum. I would have never thought a museum would need a data analyst, but this is among the country's most popular so they do have a lot of partnerships with research institutes and universities.

Transmitting Science @TransmitScience · May 29

#Job #DataAnalyst

The Field Museum (Chicago IL) is recruiting a full-time Data Analyst to **work** on **Big Data** projects for the Grainger Bioinformatics Center (GBC) of the Science and Education Department. Position for a term of 2 years.

Careers

Fueling a journey of discovery takes a diverse staff—from scientists and exhibition designers to housekeepers, educators, and accountants—work...

fieldmuseum.org

CH 8. NETWORKING, NETWORKING, NETWORKING!

Except for entry-level positions, networking is still the best way of getting a job quickly, without jumping through a million hoops. However, you must be "smart" about it, and this chapter will tell you how.

8.1 Tell your network

Whether you are a student fresh out of college, or a seasoned professional, we all have networks – our friends, family, co-workers, neighbors, and many more. So here is an easy tip – tell everyone you know that you are looking for a job. Don't be shy, don't be embarrassed, just tell them. But here is the IMPORTANT caveat, tell people what job you want.

Remember the target city and skills you searched in the second and third chapters? Use that knowledge, when you are enlisting help. Here is how a typical "ask" would look like:

Hi XXX, I am currently looking for <data scientist> roles, preferably in the <Dallas> area. My target companies are <financial> firms, but I am open to other domains/companies. If you hear of anything suitable, can you let me know?

Don't feel like you are being desperate or "cheating" or letting people down. Most people are happy to help. I once referred a girl to my manager for a data analyst position, who had not received a single job offer even 2 months after graduation, despite being quite good at coding and communicating skills. She was hired, but here is the thing – she was sent to me for mentoring by someone I respected (let's call him Mr. J), as she was his close friend's daughter. Mr. J sent her to me so I could help her with mock interviews and change her resume to the "hybrid" version. Coincidentally another manager I knew was looking to hire someone on their team, so I referred her, in part to gain brownie points with Mr. J. Networking is weird that way, it works in mysterious ways. Neither the girl's parents, nor the family friend who knew me were in the data science field, Mr. J had no idea that I would be able to refer her.

Similarly, do not scoff at your family or friends who are in fields unrelated to data science or even living across the ocean, that person might be the "bridge" to your potential hiring manager.

If you don't want your manager to know you are looking, then let your contacts know that as well.

8.2 Meetups

Meetups are a great way of meeting new people and learning new techniques in your field. However, a lot of job seekers, especially students only attend to get job leads. Some even get disrespectful if they meet a hiring manager who is not committing to give them a job. But unless the meetup is for "networking" event for hiring, assume that the relationships you build at meetups are for getting your "second" job, not the first.

Some meetups will advertise hiring events for members, hence make sure you subscribe to such alerts! At the very least add a Google notification alert for this search phrase:

"hiring event <cityname>

8.3 Career Fairs and Hiring Events

- Look for technical hiring events in your area. Most large cities have annual events. For example, PhillyTechWeek in Philadelphia has one day dedicated to job fairs.
- Companies like Deloitte, Slalom consulting sometimes have walk-in hiring events in multiple cities. However, you'd know it only if you look it up on LinkedIn.

Are you interested in a career in Finance, Supply Chain and IT? If so then make your next big move and join Deloitte in one of ten locations to learn more about a career that might be right for you. https://lnkd.in/gPAEM7x #deloitte

Deloitte Technology Networking Events

experience.deloitte.com

This is a slightly older link. However, unless you clicked the link you would never realize that the events were spread across 2 months and were being conducted in multiple cities across the US.

8.4 Other networking opportunities

- Volunteering at such events is a fantastic way of meeting potential employer as well as building your brand.

- For students, please do not miss out on any college hiring events, irrespective of what other students say. Some colleges will have different events for different majors, for example business (MBA grads) vs engineering hiring fair. Unless there is a rule against it, attend both.
- Again, if you are a student, then attend "mock interviews" by professionals who visit from large firms. Even if that company is not hiring, you may make an impression, and they could send a reference your way. This has happened to me and a couple others. At the very least, you will get genuine feedback and can prepare better for the interviews you will attend in the future.
- For students: Attend every campus event by companies, even if you think that they don't hire datascience majors, or technical folks. Believe me, all companies hire technical staff, sometimes under business domains. You don't want to miss out on a potential recruiter. In fact, you may overtake the competition because others like you, will opt out under false assumptions. For example, many people assume companies like EY, and Vanguard only hire accounting and business majors. Wrong, they have a

huge data-science department that is growing by leaps and bounds.

- If there are well-known coding bootcamps in your area, then look at their website to see who is hiring. Then apply the principles from the LinkedIn chapter, to get to know these hiring managers as you have a better shot at getting into these companies.

- Women hiring events: A lot of companies in larger cities are becoming more aware about increasing women in tech. Hence there are annual events in cities like San Francisco, Philadelphia where companies get together for a job fair targeted solely for women. Some companies also hold events on their company campus, for example JP Morgan Chase (bank) in their Wilmington, DE location. So if you are a woman looking for a new role, especially after a career break, make sure you RSVP and attend. You may not receive a job at the event, but you will get to meet directly with decision makers who can provide valuable feedback. You might also meet other working women who could potentially refer to a role in their existing company.

8.5 Don't be pushy

This brings us to the next topic, express your need for a job to everyone you know, but do not push them. If people send you leads that seem completely irrelevant (and you will receive such leads), do not get mad. Ignore the lead if you want but thank the person for thinking about you.

8.6 Internships and unpaid projects

Internships and unpaid projects don't pay money; but they can be helpful in other ways:

- You can list it as current employment
- Use the experience to build your portfolio, which is helpful to get future employment.
- Contacts to use if you need recommendations and/or present references.
- If you've been job-searching for a while, it does erode our self-confidence. In such situations, volunteering few hours per week is a good way of getting out of the house and feeling valued.

Finally remember that networking takes time, but the reward of a fabulous job is worth the effort. Also HR and hiring managers tend to favor folks who come in as referrals and such candidates also benefit from a speedier hiring process.

Ch 9. UPWORK

Upwork, to me personally is a fantastic platform, that lets you earn money, irrespective of your skill level or location. However, I realize that most people see zero results and assume it is lucrative only to contractors in Asian countries.

I've personally used Upwork for ~5 months and made $3000/month on the site, working less than 30 hours per week. It also helped me land my full-time role at Nasdaq! (recruiter came calling, honest story)

Will you earn a $100,000 on Upwork? Highly unlikely, but not impossible if you put in the time, effort and techniques listed below.

9.1 Why choose Upwork?
There are many reasons why you should consider Upwork, but here are the advantages and disadvantages.

9.1.a Advantages

- Start earning money within a week.
- Great way to build your portfolio.

- You can add "freelancer" experience, instead of showing up as "unemployed".
- Wide variety of tasks to suit your skills and expertise.
- You can increase your tax deductions (US), based on local laws.
- You can work at your own pace, fix your own schedule and be your own boss.
- No ceiling on making money.

9.1.b Disadvantages

- You do have to bid on jobs, which takes time. When you initially start, it might feel like no one is ready to give you a chance, just like no one is willing to hire. Initially, it will feel like you are overworked and underpaid.
- Upwork takes a 20% commission, from every gig, until you earn $500 from that client. To me, this feels like being looted, but sadly, you do need to pay the marketplace for bringing you a wide variety of gigs. Plus, you as a freelancer, get peace of mind since Upwork guarantees payment and will help you with disputes, if any.
- In the US, you need to pay quarterly taxes as a freelancer and fill out Schedule C (more paperwork) when you file your annual taxes. Some states (like Delaware)

you will also require a general business license, even if you don't plan to open an LLC. On the other hand, the paperwork is useful during employment verification.

9.2 Getting Started on Upwork

9.2.a Fill Your Profile

- Fill out your complete profile, like LinkedIn. Upload summary documents of your portfolio. Link to GitHub and LinkedIn.
- If you are in the US, do not keep your hourly rate below $20. Change accordingly for other countries. Keeping it artificially low makes you look desperate and good clients will wonder about the quality of work you will deliver at such ridiculous low rates. Please don't worry what potential clients will think, as the ones who want entry level work are going to pick the lowest possible number, which is beyond your control. Clients who care about getting their work done, will be happy to discuss your rate, if they like the rest of your profile.

- The way you look for jobs will be different for your first 5 gigs, versus later.

9.2.b Looking for Gigs

- Whenever you look for jobs, make sure you do not look at entry level jobs as you do not have any control over others who can underprice you.
- Do not despair over the fact, that long term hourly jobs at $50 do not exist. Your main priority is to get some work, to attract full time work, while earning money. Think of this as "pin money" to sponsor your job search.
- Hourly jobs are good. Mainly, because you can often get tasks for $20 that a good programmer can finish in 30 mins. Or a $100 project that can completed in less than 4 hours.
- Irrespective of how long you are on Upwork, you will custom reply to every gig. If you like, keep a template but customize it before hitting send. Yes, each one.
- Avoid jobs where the "hired" stat = 1. It usually means the job has been assigned, but the formalities are incomplete. No point bidding for a lost opportunity.

- Read the full job description. Some posters add special requests (like 2-hour turnaround) or local candidate requirements that might be impossible to fulfill. Some add a phrase that needs to be the first line of your message. You will be astonished how many freelancers make such avoidable mistakes.
- Sometimes you will have questions, too or a suggestion to make the project better. Put those in the reply, the client will feel happy to get a trusted and proactive consultant. If the project description is bare bones, then offer to talk about it in detail for a free 30 mins consultation. Any less than 30 mins, and you can't get enough details, anything more and you waste "billable" time.
- For every job, think through how you will tackle the task. In your bid, add the task steps and deliverables, and if possible, a sample from other similar projects. This takes longer, but you are more likely to impress the client and get hired. For example, imagine the job description says, "survey analysis" and some generic details about the number of variables and types of questions. In your

response, you can mention that you will be analyzing in R and will provide (a) summary doc in word, with insights and p-values, (b) the r program code as a textbook file, so the results can be replicated. Attach a sample report from other survey analysis with analysis on 4 variables, and maybe one moderator variable. If you've never done such an analysis, try one for practice using a free dataset from Kaggle.com or the Stack overflow developer survey or something from the bls.gov site. Then attach to your response.

- Do not hound the Clients! The employers on Upwork are typically busy entrepreneurs with limited staff and budget. If not, they would have a full-time employee working on the task. Give them a week at least to get back, and if they don't respond, then assume they hired someone else. And MOVE ON with your life.
- A hit rate of 20%-30% is normal and anything above 50% is extraordinary. By hit rate I mean, that I get hired for 2 gigs, for every 10 that I apply.

- Once you've completed 50 hours on Upwork, you can start to pick and choose what jobs you bid. At this point, you will want to get jobs that pay you at least $20-$30 per hour, so estimate the work before you bid. If you can get more, even better as this estimation will cover the hours you spend on bidding, creating proposals, etc. The more work you receive, the higher you can bid. I know freelancers who charge $1000 per project and reject invitations to anything else.
- Remember the more work you get, the higher you will rank on the site, and show up for employers who post projects. Yes, clients do get recommendations on profiles and can choose to invite such folks to bid.
- Make sure you add some of these projects in your Upwork profile, LinkedIn profile and personal website. It will help you rise in local searches on LinkedIn, too.

9.2.c Your first 5 gigs:

- The first 5 jobs are tasks you will take on to get testimonials on the site, and to show you have done some work. So, the rate does not matter.

- Tags like "rising talent" and Upwork stats only show up 90 days after you join, so you are going to mention you are new to the site in every bid.

- If you like, specify that you have listed a low rate as you want to get a high rating on the site. Clients will be happy to hire an excellent professional, that too, at a discount.

- Over-deliver. It stands to reason that you are going to complete the work before time. Thank the employer for their job, remind them to provide feedback, and ask to be considered in case any work comes up in the future.

9.2.d Pricing

You can edit the hourly or project rate, irrespective of the rate on your profile. Use the client reviews to get a sense of how much the client typically pays for similar jobs. Also look at the price ceiling for the current job. I typically take 10% off, so the clients feel they are paying less than what they budgeted. Don't discount any further, as you do not want to leave too much money on the table.

9.3 Once you get hired.

- Use the time tracker on the site to record your work, irrespective of whether it is an hourly job or prepaid project. This will discipline you to focus (no browsing the internet during work!) and help you gauge how much time projects truly take. This will help you bid better for future projects. Plus, the evidence is useful should you ever need to dispute a case with a rogue client.
- Keep the client updated on your progress every 3 days at a minimum.
- Let the client know if there are any delays or if the data shows something you had not expected when you accepted the project. Do not whine to the client, but come up with a solution as well, such as extension of the deadline, or changes to the contract. If they accept, good for you. If not, treat this as a learning opportunity and be more mindful if you need to discuss projects in more detail, for future projects.
- Give feedback to the client, with their name. This will help other freelancers, share some good karma!

In conclusion, a well-crafted response with laid out process and deliverables, a reasonable (but not ridiculously low bid) and samples will increase the client's confidence in you and want them to hire you.

Ch 10. GOOD OLD SEARCH

This chapter lists a couple of miscellaneous tactics that can help you get a job.

10.1 Startups in your area

Most job seekers want to join big name companies because of the fat paychecks and security they represent. Therefore, they fail to realize that startups and small companies are more work, but you also learn skills to boost your career. Plus, startups often have a shorter hiring cycle, which means you can start earning faster. Not to mention it is easiest to get a job when you don't need one.

You can locate these companies using the following techniques:

- Simple Google search. Look for articles in local online news websites listing the previous year's fast-growing startups. For example, a Google search for "Chicago startups":

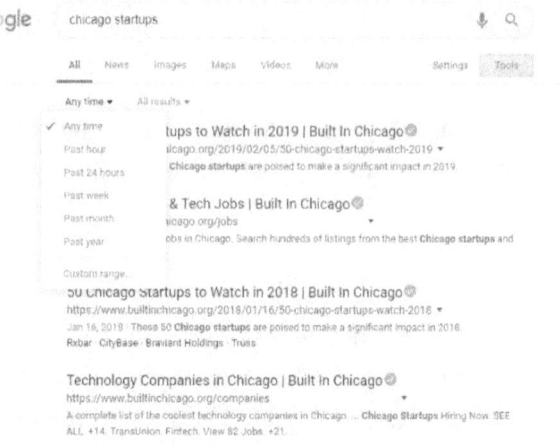

Filter by "past month" and you will see lists of top 10 companies, or local companies that are expanding furiously. "builtinchicago.com" is a site that keeps track of local companies and has a job board, too.

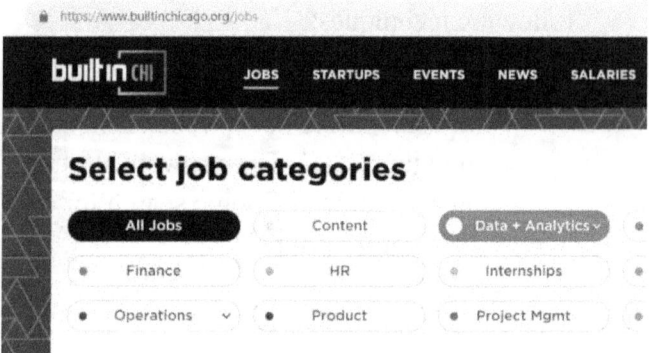

- Local newspapers (digital) will have listings of local jobs, that would not normally be advertised on larger job boards. For example, technical.ly is an online website that hosts networking meetups and job postings local to very specific cities (DC, Philadelphia, Baltimore, etc.) This article in Americaninno.com lists the hottest startups local to Chicago. There are similar sites and articles for most of the larger cities in the US, and abroad.

🔒 https://www.americaninno.com/chicago/startups-to-watch/

By Jim Dallke · December 11, 2018

CHICAGO INNO'S 19 STARTUPS TO WATCH IN 2019

Chicago's tech scene has had an eventful 2018, with major acquisitions, big funding rounds, local expansions by Silicon Valley tech giants, and of course, a failed attempt at HQ2 all generating plenty of headlines.

- Scour through the local chamber of commerce website to locate employers in your area, narrow by interest, then look up their websites. Smaller companies often post the names and contact details of hiring managers, so you may even be able to cold-email the managers directly. You have nothing to lose, and everything to gain.

10.2 Educational institutions

- Don't forget local colleges and institutions. You will have to apply online, but most job aggregators (like indeed.com or glassdoor.com) will not have these listings, so you may be able to notice a job that others do not know about. On the other hand, most colleges only post data analyst or reporting analyst type positions.

10.3 Niche job boards

Don't forget the niche job boards, specializing solely on data science jobs. Some of my favorites include:

- Kaggle.com
- DataScienceCentral.com
- KDnuggets.com
- Technical.ly Jobs – This site only caters to the US East Coast in the mid-Atlantic

area, primarily Philadelphia, Baltimore, Brooklyn/NYC, Delaware and Washington D.C.

- R-bloggers has a separate job search site called https://www.r-users.com/
- Inc.com – this is not limited to data science roles, but it does give a list of employers that you might otherwise have ignored.
- Reddit for DataScience jobs – Most users ignore it from a jobseeker perspective, but there are dedicated sub-sections only listing jobs. I would suggest using the site to scour jobs and then using the techniques listed on the LinkedIn section to make personal connections and reach out to hiring managers.
- Listing just 2 boutique recruitment agencies where friends did get placed in a rapid hiring process: (unfortunately these are US-based only)
  - Harnham recruiting,
  - Smith Hanley Associates
- Again, I repeat, do not blithely apply on the site. Instead check if there are jobs you like, and which match your skills. Next, use LinkedIn to connect with the

recruiters working at these firms and express your interest.

SECTION D – INTERVIEW PREPARATION

Ch 11. INTERVIEW PROCESS

The interview process will vary from company to company, but the most common format is as follows:

HR introductory phone call -> Hiring manager phone call -> Technical interview -> Onsite interview with manager and peers -> Salary negotiation -> Offer

With advances in technology, the format of the interview might vary. Some use Skype calls, some employers send take home tests for technical interviews, some use software for real-time coding evaluation or a combination of all the above. The sections below give a short overview along with dos and don'ts for each format.

11.1 HR/ introductory call

This will be a short call from a recruiter or HR manager and typically lasts 15-30 minutes. The main purpose of this call is to get a brief overview of your work experience and ensure there are no serious red flags in your resume.

Usually if you are not a good fit, they will let you know immediately. Otherwise, the call will normally end with the HR tell you that they will forward your resume to the hiring decision-maker.

80% of the time this will be followed by an email scheduling time for a short call with the hiring manager. The rest 20% the hiring manager may decide to go with an internal referral or decide they want somebody with more experience or a different skillset. The HR should ideally let you know either way, but if you do not hear back within a week it is perfectly acceptable to send a follow-up email. If you still do not hear back after 2 weeks, then assume the job went to someone else and move on.

If you have had a break in your career, do use this call to point it out and explain it away in 2-3 sentences. For example, you might say that you took a break to care for a parent but now you have hired a fulltime nurse and therefore are free to get back to the workforce. Moreover, you have refreshed your skills and added new ones so you will be able to hit the ground running.

New mom – be honest. Most employers understand caring for a newborn is hard work. In the US, this can also be quite expensive with daycare costs in larger cities and often the mother is the one to leave her career. So be truthful but strategic. For example, my sister mentioned how she had designed her own website and grown a personal blog to 500+ subscribers with $0 marketing, during her 5-year career break. While not relevant directly to data science it did highlight her ambition, keen business acumen and coding skills. She also mentioned the datascience certifications she had completed with flying colors and was able to receive a fabulous job offer that was 100% remote with excellent pay.

11.1.a Cautionary tale

If you have had more than 50 introductory calls but less than 5 interviews with the hiring manager, then this is a red flag for your profile. This is rare but does happen if your resume looks flaky (read lying on your resume) or if you resume looks like a job-hopper (3+ jobs staying less than 8 months per role). You may also want to look if you are applying for roles where you are considered under-qualified or over-qualified. In that case, refer to Section C (chapters 4 and 5) and apply more strategically. If possible, ask a well-wisher to conduct a mock interview and see if you are making any obvious mistakes while presenting your skills.

11.2 Hiring manager call

This will also be ~30 minutes call where the manager will tell you the basics about the role and get a sense of your work experience. If you do not make any glaring mistakes you will move on to the next stage, if you do the following:

- Truly listen to the manager and understand his expectations from this role. This is the person who might control your career, so it benefits you to listen carefully.

- Based on the description, present a short spiel about how you can fulfill all those duties. Keep it short but give examples of academic or work projects that translate well to this role. If you read the job description you should be able to answer this well.

- Do not tell the manager that you are the BEST candidate since you have no clue who else is interviewing for this role. However, you do have to sell how you are a GREAT candidate who meets all the checkboxes in terms of technical and soft skills. You cannot force the manager to hire you, but you can make it hard to find a reason to reject you.

- The manager will give you time to ask Qs. My favorite questions are listed below:
  - What is the biggest priority in this role?
  - What kinds of technical and soft skills would help a candidate excel in this role?
  - What is the one thing you love the most in this role, and one thing you dislike in this role?
  - Assume you hired me or someone else in this role, and at the end of the year you gave that person a full 5on5 rating. What would that person have accomplished to get this rating?
  - Most hiring managers are pleasantly surprised with these questions and happy to go into details. A few admit they have not really thought about it but proceed to answer. In all cases, you have shown the manager that you really are thinking about the role and adding value to the company, not just going through

the motions to get any random
high-paying job.
- o Once they finish answering,
  thank them for the insight and
  quickly use some of their points
  to reiterate how your skills and
  experience can help this
  manager accomplish their goals.
- If the manager must leave early or does
  not have time to let you ask questions,
  quickly mention that you do have
  questions and will email it to HR to pass
  it on to him. I say HR, as you rarely get
  the email address of the hiring manager.
  If you do have it offer to email it to this
  manager, so she can answer in leisure.

For this call and the HR call, make sure you will
be in a quiet place without any interruptions. Do
NOT take the call in your current employer's
phone booth rooms, a washroom (foolish but has
happened to me personally) or on the train on
your way home. Some companies do monitor
conference rooms so you might be severely
penalized for it. Take a sick day or check if you
can work from home. In the US, public libraries
have meeting rooms that can be booked in
advance.

The first 2 minutes of both calls should be used to check if the audio connection is appropriate for both parties. If this is not the case, reschedule on a later date.

Occasionally, there will be personal emergencies causing you to reschedule. If you give the HR/manager more than 2 hours' cancellation notice with a very valid reason, things will be fine. If you do need to cancel apologize profusely as they are taking time out of your busy schedule to accommodate you and now need to do it again.

11.3 Technical interviews

As a data scientist or data analyst, you must be prepared to answer technical questions. If you have put programming and software skills on your resume, you will be grilled about it.

With new software available, technical interviews can be in-person, via video conference or even collaborative. Some popular methods are listed below:

11.3.a White board

This is rare but does happen in some onsite interviews. You will be given a problem and expected to code the solution on a white board.

Remember to ask questions to understand the problem, explain the logic, which programming language you selected and talk through the code you are writing.

For most of us, writing code without an IDE editor and without looking snippets on Google is hard, so you will need to practice. Writing code on a white board in front of an audience is harder, so make sure you brush up on concepts. If needed take a look at the book "Cracking the coding interview".

11.3.b Take home tests

This is the most common scenario for data analyst and data scientist roles. You will have a deadline and most HR contacts will specify when the test question becomes available.

Dos and Donts:

- As soon as you get the email, open the attachment and check whether you can open the document/ link/ pdf. If you are sent a dropbox link, make sure you are able to download a copy. This seems like common sense, but I have seen candidates who received the link on Friday afternoon and only opened it on Sunday night to realize that the link was broken or valid only for 24 hours. HR can enable the link again, but this reflects badly on the candidate since we know they are not serious about this position.

- Use the full available time. Most exams state how much time they will take, but you might be different. The earlier you start, the more time you have to polish things up. Remember you don't need to say you spent the whole week doing the assignment.

- Irrespective of whether a summary document is asked or not, provide one. Data analysis is just one part of the role. Cleaning messy data, exploring it and providing final recommendations for action are equally important parts. Show your employer how you can decipher meaningful insights and present them in a concise and compelling way.

- If you are getting a chance to present this code in a scheduled onsite interview, then this summary doc will be helpful to build a ppt doc and an outline for your talk.

11.3.c Code walk-through

For entry level roles, managers may ask you to present a project of your choice and walk them through the code. This feels scary but we only want to check whether you have basic analytics competency. Allowing the candidate to choose the project is meant to make the session less stressful.

- If you can, present something unique. Not Titanic or bike sharing data.
- If possible, present something that is relevant to the company you are interviewing with. For my interview with Nasdaq I created an interactive Tableau-style dashboard using R presenting stock price movements for the largest companies in their proprietary QQQ portfolio. For a media company, I tracked and pulled Twitter follower counts (using Twitter API) and showed how recent viral articles caused their follower counts to spike and ebb.
- This takes extra effort, but it will help you stand out immensely.
- Practice. Present to a friend or senior family member and prepare for possible questions.

11.3.d Collaborative editor

These are gaining in popularity, but they do feel stressful even for senior developers. The concept is that you will be writing code in a video call with screenshare, and the interviewer can see what you are doing.

Depending on the software you may or may not be able to use Google or Stack overflow. Having someone virtually watch over your shoulder does feel weird, but you may not have an option.

Typically, not used for entry-level roles, but I am seeing these interviews become standard for experienced data scientist hires.

11.3.e Online coding exams

If the role entails SQL and/or Python, then you may be sent a link to give a coding exam. These are normally timed exams. From my personal experience, most of these are medium to easy, if the candidate does not get stuck on a question. The editor generally does not auto complete, and you cannot test your code, which is a major handicap to most interviewees.

Again, practice in Notepad and then run the code in IDE to get better with your coding skills.

11.4 Case Study Analysis

This will be a part of the interview process only for consulting companies or for roles with high visibility. The "Vault" guide is an old book from

2007, but the concepts are still valid. Download and store as another technique in your arsenal. You can either Google it, or download it from the link http://questromworld.bu.edu/clubconsulting/files /2010/09/Vault-Guide-to-the-Case-Interview-2008-more-cases-1.pdf

11.5 Onsite interviews

If you made it to the onsite office interview stage, congratulations! You are much closer than the rest of the competition. If the hiring manager finds you reasonably competent and you do not make any glaring mistakes, you have a good chance of getting hired.

Onsite interviews last between 3 hours to a full day and the objective is to evaluate the candidate by multiple interviewers. One will be the manager or his peer, one interview with a senior manager, one with someone outside the group (for objectivity) and one optionally with folks who are peers or junior to the role. An interview with HR (again) is also possible.

Dos and Don'ts:

- You may get asked to walk through your resume again and again. Do not get annoyed or impatient. Display courtesy and grace for all the interviews.

- You may get asked the same behavioral question repeated by every interviewer. It might be coincidence or a shrewd tactic to see if you keep changing answers.
- It is perfectly acceptable to ask questions in return. Read section 11.2 for sample questions.

11.5.a Stress test

You may be faced with 2 or more interviewers where they fire questions at you and give very little time to answer. This is common for cross-functional roles and in consulting companies, to evaluate how you fare under pressure.

Be cool and answer patiently.

11.5.b Panel interview

Multiple interviewers, single candidate. The questions will not seem as interrogative as a stress interview but being alone with so many senior folks can be intimidating. This type of interview includes panel presentation and technical interviews.

11.5.c Lunch interview

Treat this the same as an interview in an office.

- Do not order items that will be difficult or messy to eat. This is still an interview and you do not want to talk with your mouth full.
- Do not order alcohol, even if the interview asks or orders one for themselves. [I should not even need to mention this, but I have seen candidates make this mistake repeatedly.]
- Be respectful.
- Feel free to ask the interviewer (or a team) questions about his role, what they enjoy about the company, culture, etc.
- Do not ask about compensation, educational reimbursement or any other type of compensation.
- Do not talk politics or religion, unless the interviewer broaches those topics.

11.6 Skype interview/ Video conference

Alternatives to onsite and phone interviews.

- Make sure you are dressed well and in a clean room with good lighting.
- Ideal would be to have a large blank wall behind you.
- If you are taking the video call in your home, lock the door to ensure no one accidentally walks in or disturbs you.

- If the HR accepts, offer to connect 15 minutes prior to the call to test the connection. I once had an interview where the video in their office was extremely grainy. I could see them, but they could not, so everything had to be moved back by an hour until their tech support fixed the issue. Unfortunately, this meant I had to be on call for most of the extra hour, so the technician could ensure my video was coming through.
- If you have back-to-back video conferences, then ensure that the interviewer does not cut the connection. Ask each new interviewer if they can see and hear you without difficulty.

Now that you have understood the different types of interviews, let us dive into the next chapter with real-life questions.

Ch 12. INTERVIEW QUESTIONS

You optimized your profile, you connected with managers and now you have an interview call with a good company. Here are 100+ interview questions to help you prepare for those meetings. The questions below are sorted logically into sections, although some questions can fall into multiple sections.

12.1 Behavioral Qs:

1. Tell me about yourself.
    Most interviewers use this as an icebreaker and to see how well you communicate. So please do not use it as an excuse to ramble on your life story. A great answer would quickly describe your experiences up to this point, explain why you are a fit. If possible, you should (optional) throw in a memorable trivia about you so the interview has a clear memory hook to remember you among all the interviewees he meets for that role. **IMPORTANT REMINDER** – Every interview question should be answered with one main goal: how do you show that you will add value to the manager

and his team? Prepare for every question to show how the employer benefits from hiring you, not what you expect to gain.

2. Why are you interested in Data Science? If you do not have a technical background, then this is just to gauge whether you are truly interested or simply here for the money, and therefore liable to quit if things get hectic.

3. Describe how you overcame a challenge in your work.
   For any behavioral question, use the STAR technique to present your answer.
   S – Situation. Short background
   T – Task. What was the goal?
   A – Action. What steps did you take?
   R – Results. What happened at the end, as a result of your action? Ideally the results should **always** reflect positively on you, but if you do decide to use a neutral story, do add comments to say what you learnt from the situation and how it has helped you in later situations.

4. How do you approach a project?
   This is basically to check your logical thinking abilities and to gauge whether

you can work without supervision and constant handholding.

5. What do you do for fun?
   This sounds like an icebreaker question, but this question is also used to gauge whether you are a cultural fit. Unless the company is a liberal startup or known for an extremely casual atmosphere, please keep your answers conservative. Do your homework on the company and try to make sure that you fit the persona of an ideal company. Disclaimer – this is not an invitation to lie, please do NOT do that. If you truly think you are not a cultural fit, then treat the interview experience as an experiment and reflect seriously whether you would want to work in that company, should you be offered the role.
   For data engineer and senior scientist roles, it is perfectly acceptable to be "geeky" and talk about a pet software project you are building.

6. Pick up a project from your resume/GitHub which had a great impact. OR tell me about an interesting data science project.

If you read the initial chapters, then you should have some interesting projects on hand to talk about. Even entry-level data analysts can get asked this question, so be prepared. You do not need a super original idea, but you do need to present your unique take on the subject. The expectation is that you show (1) you can write decent code which is well-documented. (2) you know how to present your findings and have acceptable communication skills.

7. Being from electrical/economic/bioscience background, why do you want to join as a data analyst?
   Similar expectations as Q2.

8. Why are you looking for a new job?
   "I am unemployed/ broke/ desperate/hate my current employer / hate my current manager." are all wrong answers. Even if you are in this situation, you do not need to vent it to your future manager. If you are a student or parent returning to the workforce, be honest. Otherwise say something neutral along the lines of 'looking for new growth opportunities.

- If a recruiter reached out on LinkedIn, say truthfully that you are not actively looking, but you found this specific job listing interesting.
- If you have had multiple jobs in the last 4 years, be aware that the hiring manager is trying to judge if you are a "job hopper". Millennials have received this unnecessary stereotype, so there may be an unconscious bias at play. In such cases it is acceptable to say that you are not actively looking, just answering very specific roles. Then explain how the job fits your experiences and how you can add value.

9. How do you find out trending queries/topics? Finding if you take initiative and keep your skills/knowledge updated.
Each person will answer differently, but some decent answers include Coursera, Udemy, Forbes magazines, Wall street journal, websites like KDnuggets.

Datascience roles all involve technology, and those change rapidly. Hence you should have an answer. Do not state you are so busy that you have not had time to keep updated with new skills.

10. What are your coding pet peeves?
Keep it short and simple like badly documented code or library packages that are not well-maintained. Don't elaborate as interviews should be kept as positive as possible.

11. Are you a team player or an individual contributor?
The correct answer is both, irrespective of what the role entails. You need to be self-motivated to do your tasks well and within deadlines. Yet, no team works in a silo, so you do need to have good team skills.

12.2 Product Companies - Facebook, LinkedIn, Uber

If you are interviewing for product-based companies like Facebook, Uber, Shopify or even banking companies, then please do a thorough research on what the company does, its products, new and recent launches, latest company news, changes in the executive team, and so on. It is a BAD idea to be ignorant about the company and ask these when the interview gives you time to pose questions back.

12. Metrics to measure success/failure of one Facebook product.
    This question is used to assess your logical thinking and your familiarity with the products.
    Use that knowledge to pose some basic metrics (product downloads, increase in per customer LTV, reduction in churn, etc.) and KPIs, basic A/B testing and KPI monitoring.

13. Suppose FB wants to launch feature X on product Y - how would you assess whether this is a good idea? How about when standard AB Testing does not work?
    Similar to above.

14. What do you think are Deliveroo/ GrubHub/ Stripe's biggest costs?

If you studied the company well, you should be able to make an educated guess. State your answer along with your logic. If necessary, the interviewer can correct you.

Datascience roles exist so that companies can increase profits, either by (1) reducing costs and improving process efficiency, or (2) by earning more per customer and increasing the number of customers. Your answer will reveal whether you are able to look beyond coding and grasp what is truly vital to the company – the "whys" of data analysis.

15. Would you rather take on a more technical role, or focus on business problems? What would your ideal project be like?

The perfect answer will depend on the job description, and from the role description the manager provided (if any). Ideally you would say you are good in both roles, and then choose the side that matches the description. If you are interviewing for a role that is the opposite to what you secretly prefer, reflect if you will really be happy in the role.

16. What statistical techniques would you use in xyz scenario?
Lay out your thinking process verbally, so the interviewer can correct if you are making a false assumption. For a cheat sheet on machine learning algorithms and common statistical techniques, refer to the links in chapter 3, section 3.5

17. How would you measure the health of Mentions, Facebook's app for celebrities? How can FB determine if it's worth it to keep using it? If a celebrity starts to use Mentions and begins interacting with their fans more, what part of the increase can be attributed to a celebrity using Mentions, and what part is just a celebrity wanting to get more involved in fan engagement?
Like Q12 and 13 of this section.

18. How would you prioritize which country to expand Slack to for furthering the International effort?
To answer this Q, you will need to know which the current markets are for the company and choose an emerging market (South America or China or smaller tech

hubs in Europe). Explain why you chose
the answer. Note, the company already
has a base in India.

19. Difference between FB and Twitter
    graphs.

20. How will you define a metric that
    measures skewness of the network?

21. Lyft/ Uber - What are the different
    factors that could influence a rise in
    average wait time of a driver?

22. What would you improve with the Uber/
    LinkedIn/ Candy crush app?
    This question tests both your familiarity
    with the product and your business
    acumen. Unless you are a loyal user, you
    will not really be able to answer this
    question.

23. If you were made the first data scientist at
    Spirit Airlines/ Apple/ Nike where would
    you start?
    Similar to Q22.
    The first data science teams wear many
    hats and data collection is the biggest
    challenge, so it is a good idea to explain

how you can handle ambiguity and think out-of-the-box.

24. You have been tasked with creating a prediction for the outcome of the 2014 congressional elections. You are responsible for building your own dataset for this process.
This was a question for the company "Civis analytics" which helps business with customized targeting of new users and increase the lifetime value of existing users. So, this question is perfect to understand whether the candidate truly understands the company's work or not.

25. Build a model to match the JD of a candidate with the CV. Or how would you design a platform like Amazon/Airbnb/LinkedIn.
All questions related to building a recommender system, i.e. a matchmaking engine. Reply with both business metrics to assess feasibility and the machine learning engines that can generate the best results. Feel free to ask questions regarding data sources, starting from an initial MVP (minimum viable product), intermediate and final version.

12.3 Machine Learning Qs:

Many interviewers will ask you about very specific machine learning algorithms or ask you to explain your favorite algorithm. Be prepared with a basic answer on each including the following points:

- Basic algorithm working
- Best use case or application
- pros and cons

26. Explain Survival Analysis.

27. What is PCA? Where is it used?

28. Describe the pros and cons of different neural network structures that could be used for natural language processing.

29. What is confusion matrix for multiclass classification?

30. How do you evaluate a model after training?
Start your explanation using metrics of accuracy, precision, recall, etc.

31. What can go wrong when training a classifier?
Answer should explain skewed samples, overfitting, etc.

32. Can you use a random forest classifier to perform regression?

33. Explain clustering by elaborating one clustering algorithms.
Typically talk about K-means algorithm.

34. What is the most important thing for the successful data project?
Answer should explain an understanding of pulling business requirements, evaluation metrics, accurate data and applying the optimal algorithm.

35. How to avoid overfitting in neural network?

36. Explain difference between supervised and unsupervised machine learning algorithms.

37. What are the advantages and disadvantages of Gradient Boosted

Models/ random forest / neural networks/ others?

38. How do you use clustering in text mining?

39. Explain how to handle noisy data?

40. Handling Unstructured data?

41. What is CNN, RNN?

42. Show to use SVD for performing PCA.

43. Describe 2 or 3 examples of applications of Machine learning & AI on the typical data collected from the company customers (customer journey).

44. You are about to get on a plane to Seattle. You want to know if you should bring an umbrella. You call 3 random friends of yours who live there and ask each independently if it's raining. Each of your friends has a 2/3 chance of telling you the truth and a 1/3 chance of messing with you by lying. All 3 friends tell you that "Yes" it is raining. What is the probability that it is raining in Seattle?

This is a classic Bayesian analysis, although if you want to apply basic probability, you may go that route. Just explain your logic and thought process out loud, instead of blurting out the final answer.

45. FB has hired raters to rate ads. 80% are careful rates and rate 60% of the ads as good and 40% as bad, 20% are lazy raters and rate 100% ads as good. What is the probability that an ad is rated good? Given that 3 ads have been rated as good, what is the probability that they were rated by a lazy rater? Given that n ads have been rated as good, what is the probability that they were rated by a lazy rater? You want to classify raters as careful/lazy; how would you do that using all the probabilities and ideas discussed above (open ended question)? Explain your thought process; the problem-solving approach is more important than the final answer.

46. Where does the randomness come from for a random forest algorithm?

47. How would you build a system to rank the potential of a large group of sales contacts?
Same vein as Q45.

48. Verbally construct a naive bases algorithm for predicting the color of a card, given provided sets of conditional probabilities

49. How would you deal with imbalanced classes in a machine learning context? This question is quite common in teams dealing with fraud analysis, customer churn and survival analysis.

50. What kind of data structure would you use in R to store key-value pairs?

51. How do you set up and model this survival analysis problem using hypothetical patient data?
Another question to check problem solving skills. Remember to start with your basic understanding of the problem, common sense assumptions and initial metrics to build the system. Keep the interviewer involved with your thought process and ask questions. If they do not

answer, simply state and say these are the constraints you are choosing and keep going.

52. Bias-variance tradeoff. explain.

53. How to select the important features from the set of 1000 variable.

54. Explain instability in decision tree and how rotation affects decision tree model?

55. Develop an algorithm for client segmentation.

12.4 Logic / Coding:

56. What insights do you get from the given dataset?

57. Describe how to calculate the return of an investment based on two scenarios. Provide some analysis on the non-economical pros and cos of each approach.

58. There was a univariate weekly data. How will you forecast data for the next 3 weeks? The next one year?

You can use your preferred time series forecasting method. You can also use the STL decomposition approach in R programming.

59. Somebody asks you for advice when it comes to a classification problem. An 80% classification accuracy was found. What do you think about that? Is it good / bad? What advice would you give?

60. You are compiling a report for user content uploaded every month and notice a spike in uploads in October. You see a spike in picture uploads. What might you think is the cause of this, and how would you test it?
Answer should suggest October events like Halloween (US), Diwali (India). This is essentially a trick question to evaluate whether you apply basic business acumen as well as technical analysis.

61. How do you proof that males are on average taller than females by knowing just gender or height?

62. On a scale from 1 to 10, how would you rate your SQL/Python/R/Tableau skills?

Try not to answer anything below a 7. Do not answer 10 either, as there is always a new library or approach that you will be unaware of.

63. What algorithm will you use on a dataset?

64. How to identify the missing values in a data set?

65. Explain hyperparameters in different sklearn models

66. Code the game of life.
If you do not know about the game, ASK. Start with the basic requirements and only then start to code your answer.

67. How do you get the count of each letter in a sentence?

68. How do you test whether a new credit risk scoring model works?

69. How to handle big, sparse data set?

70. What are the assumptions of linear regression?

71. What is probability of getting one pair of cards from 52 deck of cards?

72. How to sort a list?

73. How to penalize seasonality and periods in a model?
    If the role entails time series data, then this is an expected question.

74. How would you develop a model to predict ticket pricing? What features would you use? How do you deal with missing data, bad data, too much data etc.

75. Find the least possible 10-digit prime number which is a palindrome?

76. Given the set of integers, find all the pairs that yields the specific sum.

77. What is the difference between bucketing and partitioning?

78. Would you prefer train-test or train-test-validation? Why?

79. How would you test if survey responses were filled at random by certain individuals, as opposed to truthful selections?

80. What is statistical measure?

81. What is AUC?

82. Brain teaser: If you have 100 marbles (Half of them red and half black) and you are given two jars to fill them. How would you fill the jars so that you can maximize the chances of someone picking a red marble when they randomly choose one of the two jars?

83. What is a statistical method to control the number of features for large sparse matrices?

84. How do you test a website feature i.e. given a set of webpages and few changes, how will you find out that the change works positively? A/B testing.

85. Explain shortest path - maze problem.

86. The interview drew a hypothetical histogram of number of purchases per user. There are a lot of users that make a small number of purchases, and few users that make many purchases. So, the histogram is peaked near zero and has a tail off to the left. Based on this, what do you expect the plot of average revenue per user to look like?

87. Cistern and Pipes problem.

88. A certain array contains only 0's and 1's, can you segregate the 0's and 1's by traversing the array only once?

89. Why do we use sigmoid and not any increasing function from 0 to 1?

90. What is cross entropy?

91. How do you draw a uniform random sample from a circle in polar coordinates?

92. what is stationary signal?

93. Given a table of users, dates, statuses, etc. - calculate the ratio X grouped by Y on day Z. Call out edge cases - don't assume anything without clarifying.

94. Given a random Bernoulli trial generator, write a function to return a value sampled from a normal distribution.

95. Where to use Median OR Mean?

96. Difference between a Z test and a T test.

97. Explain P-value.

98. Type -1 and 2 errors. Explain with examples.

99. How do you deal with fat-tailed distributions?

100.　　　Why did you choose MCMC to solve a problem? Do you know any other MC algorithms?

12.6 SQL questions

Refer Chapter 3.

12.7 Python programming questions
****

Refer Chapter 3.

12.8 R programming questions
****

Refer Chapter 3.

Ch 13. SOME MORE ADVICE...

The techniques listed in this book will help you find a data science job quickly. Job-hunting is a fulltime job and can be quite demotivating. Believe in yourself, do not let your coding skills get rusty.

At the same time, don't be too demanding. Competition for data science jobs is fierce, especially at the lower levels. At first, if you don't get a job in your dream company, don't fret. You can switch in 6-8 months. Again, it is easiest to get a job when you already have one. (as quoted by dozens of recruiters and hiring managers). Don't foolishly reject a $4,000 job and waste months in the hopes of getting a $10,000 job that may or may not materialize. The techniques in this book will help you even if you already have a job, so you can continue looking outside office hours.

Thank you for reading this book and wish you the very best in your job search!

[Don't forget to leave a review on Amazon – your feedback is extremely important to me!]

CH 14. ALL BONUS CONTENT HERE..

14.1 New Niche Sites

Two recent alternatives to job search platforms are:

- Keyvalues.com – This site mostly has startups and companies in growth phase, but I did see a lot of remote positions. They also have some interesting product companies which claim to be 100% family friendly, meaning if you need to attend a function at your child's school, you can. For some people, values are as important as salary and this site will help those that do.

- WorkataStartup – This site is the hiring portal for companies associated with YC Combinator, a world-renowned startup incubator. Most of the jobs relate to software engineering or sales, but I did see a couple of data scientist and data engineer roles, too. It is more of a matching engine between companies and applicants, and the roles are mandatorily at small growing companies. Plus, you have the opportunity to work at a startup which at least has the potential to become the next Uber or Airbnb.

- AngelList – Noticed I had not included this site for startup jobs. I used it couple years ago, and mostly saw CTO/biz dev and software roles, and very few datascience roles. However, that has changed a lot and now the site has multiple jobs for data analyst/ manager/ scientist. I saw roles from India, US, LatAm and many where the role allows 100% remote work.

About the Author

Anupama Rajaram (aka Ann) is award-winning analytics professional with experience working with Financial giants like NASDAQ, TD bank and BlackRock. She is currently a manager in the credit card fraud analytics team for TD North America. She lives with her family in Delaware, USA and enjoys traveling, reading and blogging on her website www.journeyofanalytics.com She is passionate about promoting women in STEM.

Follow her on Twitter at anu_analytics or on LinkedIn at
https://www.linkedin.com/in/anupamaprv/

One Last Thing...

If you enjoyed this book or found it useful, I'd really appreciate if you could post a short review on Amazon.

Your feedback really does make a difference and can help others land their dream job in the exciting field of data science. I personally read all the reviews so your honest opinion will make this book even better.

Thanks again for your support!